Instructor's Resource Guide

for

Counseling and Psychotherapy
A Multicultural Perspective

Fourth Edition

Allen E. Ivey
University of Massachusetts, Amherst

Mary Bradford Ivey
Amherst Regional Schools
University of Massachusetts, Amherst

Lynn Simek-Morgan
Florida International University

Allyn and Bacon
Boston · London · Toronto · Sydney · Tokyo · Singapore

A Viacom Company
160 Gould Street
Needham Heights, Massachusetts 02194

Internet: www.abacon.com
America Online: keyword: College Online

ISBN 0-205-26745-9

Printed in the United States of America

10 9 8 7 6 5 4 3 2 1   01 00 99 98 97 96

CONTENTS

Section I	Sequencing Chapters		vi
Section II	Suggestions for Teaching Each Chapter		1
	1	The Culturally Intentional Counselor or Therapist: Introduction and Overview	1
	2	Emphatic Attitude: Individual, Family, and Culture	9
	3	Conducting an Intentional Interview: Theory, Skills, Decisions, and Solutions	18
	4	Developmental Counseling and Therapy: Integrating Individual and Family Perspectives *Includes instrument for assessing cognitive-developmental level.*	30
	5&6	Multicultural Counseling and Therapy I and II: Metatheory—Taking Theory into Integrative Practice *Includes transcript of feminist counseling interview.*	51
	7	Psychodynamic Counseling and Therapy, Part I: Conception and Theory	69
	8	Psychodynamic Counseling and Therapy, Part II: Applications for Practice *Includes transcript of psychodynamic interview*	84
	9	Cognitive-Behavioral Therapy and Counseling I: Behavioral Foundations	100
	10	Cognitive-Behavioral Therapy and Counseling II Cognitive and Integrative Approaches	111
	11	The Existential-Humanistic Tradition I: Existential-Humanistic Theory and Practice	123
	12	The Existential-Humanistic Tradition II Logotherapy and Experiential Gestalt Therapy *Includes transcript of modification of attitudes interview*	132
	13	Toward an Integrated Counseling and Psychotherapy	145
Section III	Portfolio of Competencies		147
Section IV	Example Course Syllabus		153
Section V	Final Examination and Final Paper/Transcript *Includes Study Guide, Scoring Suggestions, and Specifics of how to development an interview transcript*		166

Preface

This Instructor's Manual is designed to accompany *Counseling and Psychotherapy: A Multicultural Perspective* (4th Edition). In this manual, we try to share some of the ideas that have been helpful to us in teaching this course to graduate students and to advanced undergraduates.

Features of this manual include the following sections:

Alternative chapter sequences for teaching the course.

Materials for teaching

Overview of Chapter
Class Procedures
Multiple Choice Questions
Essay Questions
Suggested Supplementary Reading

Supplementary case transcripts which may be duplicated for students illustrating special concepts. Several case examples are included in the Chapter instructional material.

Portfolio of competencies. This part of the course we could not recommend more highly. We find that students master theory best by actually practicing the exercises. When I teach the course, I like students able to demonstrate that they can use the theories. The book contains many exercises which help students take theory into practice. Students typically present their portfolios at the end of the term with great pride. Not only have they learned theory, they have learned how to practice and apply the theory.

Example Course Syllabus This is a rather lengthy outline with a focus on counseling and therapy competencies to be achieved as well as cognitive mastery.

Final examination including study guide and scoring suggestions. The examination is designed as an integrative exercise for the entire text.

These materials are designed so that the instructor can adapt and change them. There are more ideas and concepts than you will need or want. Hopefully, some of these will be useful and/or spark even better ideas on your part. In future guides, I would enjoy including and crediting your ideas for teaching an effective course.

This teacher manual is available on disk and that may be helpful to those of you who, like me, have a setting unable to offer sufficient secretarial assistance. In doing an exam, for example, you can cut and paste items you like. Perhaps even more important, if you don't like the way item stems are written, you can change them to fit the needs of your group. You may want to use portions of the Portfolio of Competencies or part or the sample Syllabus. If you wish to have a copy on disk, write me at 2 Cranberry Lane, Amherst, MA 01002. Please send a stamped self-addressed envelope, a formatted disk, suitable for Macintosh™ computers, and I'll send a copy of the disk suitable for Word™ 5.1.

Supporting videotapes. Over the years, I have worked with Microtraining Associates to generate videotapes presenting issues in counseling and psychotherapy. These tapes include a variety of materials useful for classroom instruction. Most include role-play demonstrations of concepts in this book. Among them are: 1) three excellent lectures on multicultural counseling and therapy by Derald Wing Sue; 2) a series of multicultural tapes on counseling African-Americans (Thomas Parham), Asian-Americans (Derald Sue), Latina/o's (Patricia Arredondo), and Native American Indians (Teresa La Fromboise); 3) Paul Pedersen on multicultural counseling issues; 4) issues in counseling women by Norma Gluckstern and Mary Ivey (which features a very interesting discussion of African-American women's issues by Jean Moss); 5) George Gazda on group counseling; 6) Norman Kagan on Interpersonal Process Recall (very useful with the empathic conditions chapter and the psychodynamic chapter); 7) microskills of Chapter 3 including demonstration of the five-stage interview of decisional counseling used throughout the text. New is a solution-oriented demonstration tape; 8) developmental counseling and therapy concepts useful with Chapters 4 and the discussion of developmental personality styles of the psychodynamic chapters; 9) a dream analysis tape, coupled with a logotherapy and assertiveness training demonstration. Other materials are forthcoming, many with a multicultural focus. Contact: Microtraining Associates, Inc., Box 641, North Amherst, MA 01059 for information on these materials.

A word about style. This material has an inconsistent style. I started writing with the impersonal "we" and about half way through I found myself "getting into" the task more and I shift to "I statements." I hope you'll pardon the change in style and take my enthusiasm with a grain of salt. I was elected to write the manual. It isn't perfect, but I hope you will find some ideas and materials which are useful.

Again, we'd welcome hearing from you with your ideas and reactions. Best wishes for a great course with some wonderful students.

Allen Ivey

Section I

The Issue of Sequencing

There are many ways to sequence a course on counseling and psychotherapy. A frequently used sequence is presented in the text. That sequence is based on the concept of foundation skills and multicultural counseling and therapy (MCT) followed by the traditional first, second, and third forces. Integration of theories closes the text. I've taught the course in that order and it seems to work.

A critical issue may be, however, that is might be useful to present the first three forces of psychology first and then conclude with integrative MCT metatheory. The text is organized so that multiple approaches to sequencing is possible. Many of us like to change the order of the text to meet varying needs of student groups. Here are some possibilities:

1. Beginning Students with Minimal Experience in Foundational Skills. I often teach a combined course in which advanced human services students are mixed with beginning masters and a very few younger doctoral students. I give more time to the Foundational skills than I would to more advanced groups. This group, to me, seems to require more time on foundational skills and thus I reorder the course as follows:

> Foundational Skills (Chapters 1 and 13 [for overview of course], 2, 3, 4) If students master the competencies and skills of these early chapters, I find that they are able to master the later chapters at a much higher level.
> Rogers and Frankl (Chapters 10 and 11) This is to ensure that students have a solid footing in listening skills and the traditional humanistic orientation.
> MCT (5 and 6)
> Psychodynamic (7-8)
> Cognitive-Behavioral Therapy (9-10)
> Integration of Skills (13)

An example syllabus for this sequence may be found in this teacher manual.

2. For Students Who Have Completed Prior Courses in Skills and Empathic Conditions. In this situation, I recommend less time on the Foundational Theories, but still emphasizing the multicultural components (the community genogram of Chapter 1 and the family heritage exercise of Chapter 2). In addition, students will find the introduction to solution-oriented methods helpful. Developmental counseling and therapy concepts will be useful in helping even advanced students work more successfully with the demanding exercises of the later chapters. The extra time this allow will permit more time on MCT and the other theories of helping. You may want to add the Assessment Chapter from this Guide as described in the Preface.

3. Advanced Students Emphasizing Multicultural Issues. With this group, I would first emphasize the community and family genogram of Chapters 1 and 2. Then, I would start with the chapters on MCT and Therapy and then view all other materials through that lens. Assignments would focus on examining all the chapters from a combined family/multicultural focus. *The individual develops in a family in a culture.* The Assessment Chapter from this Guide as described in the Preface may be helpful.

4. Two-Semester Sequence. With supplementary reading from original sources, this text can easily fill a year-long or two-quarter course. The emphasis on the Portfolio of Competencies, in particular, provides an opportunity for students to master both theory and practice.

In short, there are many reasonable sequences for a course of this type. I am sure you have many more ideas of your own. Each population is different—adapt and change materials to fit your views and the students needs.

Section II

Suggestions for Teaching Each Chapter

Chapter 1

The Culturally Intentional Counselor and Therapist: Introduction and Overview

Overview

This chapter defines the key constructs underlying this book. The central ideas are defined as:

1. *Worldview.* The way you and your clients make sense of things depends on your way of making *meaning* in the world. Each individual makes unique meanings, but these meanings also have universal human qualities.

2. *Cultural intentionality.* While we are all unique humans, we are also influenced by multicultural factors. It is critical that you develop awareness in yourself and others of how issues such as race/ethnicity and gender affect the way you and your clients construct meaning in the world.

3. *The scientist-practitioner.* Counseling and psychotherapy is not just opinion. The field rests on a scientific base. It is our task as responsible clinicians and counselors to draw on research as we plan our interventions.

4. *Ethics.* All our helping interventions rest on a moral base. You as a counselor or therapist will be constantly called on to make ethical decisions. Effective practice is ethical practice.

5. *Theory into Practice—The Community Genogram.* This is a book which focuses on taking ideas into concrete action. The community genogram is a practice strategy which will make it possible for your students to have a specific strategy for the interview during the first week of the course. In addition, the community genogram helps students see their clients in social and cultural context.

Class Procedures

1. Relativity and worldview. I like to begin class with a focus on the students themselves and their ideas and feelings with the goal of pointing out to them that they bring considerable understanding and expertise to the field. At the same time, I like to help students realize there are many ways to make sense of the fields of counseling and psychotherapy, that they need to take an active part in that definition, and that the field is still growing and changing.

One exercise I like is showing a videotape of a client and asking students to write down how they would like to respond to that client and how they conceptualize the client's problem. I then have them divide into groups and discuss their observations. A group report-out follows and I am always amazed at how differently the members of the class would respond and how differently they view the client's problem.

With knowledge that they see the same event differently, I move to the Escher print and discuss with them the ideas of relativity and worldview.

As time permits, we like to examine the different styles of worldview presented in the text and ask them to generate additional theoretical worldviews of their own. Ultimately, it is each student who will decide and this is a good place to help them see their responsibility to themselves and to others.

2. The Four Building Blocks of a Worldview. Counseling and therapy have been traditionally thought of as individual issues with underlying universal dimensions. The idea that family and cultural factors may be as important in helping theory is relatively new. We find it important to discuss this point with students in some detail. Each person is unique, but is part of universal humanity; moreover family history so closely defines us and it is in the family that we can most easily see and understand cultural history.

3. Cultural Intentionality. It is helpful to present each key point of intentionality with an example. We like to start with the class brainstorming examples of stuckness or lack of intentionality. We then take some of these specific examples and generate positive examples of intentionality for each of the three aspects of the definition. Examples are provided in the text.

4. Post-Modernism and Stories. New to this edition is working specifically with client stories from a narrative frame of reference. While narrative theory is not stressed in this text, it and social constructivist ideas are imbedded throughout. The post-modern frame of reference is discussed in more detail in Chapter 4 on developmental counseling and therapy.

A useful exercise is to ask your class members to divide into small groups and suggest that they tell stories about the community in which they grew up. After the stories have been shared, ask them how this story may affect them today in the ways they think and feel about themselves and their world. What parts of them represent continuation of community stories—or perhaps what parts of them represent an effort to work against past community experiences and stories? What stories would someone else tell about their communities?

5. Spirituality and Religion. This new material was added because of a question asked in my multicultural course—"How many of you have spirituality and religion as an important part of your support system?" In a rather secular university, I found 60% of the students looked to this area for support.

The classroom exercise is parallel to that above. Ask some variation of the question I asked and then ask students in small groups to explore how spirituality and religion might be part of a culturally-sensitive counseling and therapy.

6. The Community Genogram. The genogram is a useful homework exercise. You may wish to demonstrate its use in the class. A video entitled *Psychotherapy as Liberation* contains a demonstration of the community genogram and is available from Microtraining Associates at the address in the introductory materials of this Instructor Resource Guide.

7. The Scientist-Practitioner. It is helpful if students are introduced early to the importance of research in the counseling process early. A useful assignment is to have them examine a professional journal article and write a one to two page summary of the implications of the research piece for counseling and therapy theory and practice.

You may have one of your own favorite articles which you want them to review and examine. In some cases, class research projects can be assigned here.

8. Ethics. This is not a book on ethics, but ethical practice must undergird all that we do. At a minimum it seems important in this course to:

a. Discuss the Korman quote and the General Guidelines for Providers of Professional services on multicultural issues and ethical practice. You may want to inform your students that it has taken some time for this quotation to be taken seriously and their implications for the field at this time.

b. The relational vs. individual orientation needs to be stressed as this point reappears throughout the book. We like to present individual case examples and then ask students how the client problem might be resolved from an individual and from a relational orientation. Students need to learn that the focus on "I statements" usually represents the individual orientation whereas "we statements" more closely approximate the relational view of the world.

c. Outline the key ethical points and add any others that you consider important. As our classes so often involve practice sessions and students may self-disclose personal issues, we ask students to generate their own code of ethics for this course and write personal and group statements on this important issue.

Multiple Choice Questions.

1. Escher's print *Relativity* is used in the text to point out that

a) what is real depends on perspective.*
b) point out all counseling is relative.
c) the perspective we chose in counseling must be clearly defined.
d) different theories of counseling think about the world differently.

2. Worldview may be defined as

a) the meaning different theories give to the same client experience and that meaning will likely vary from theory to theory.
b) the meaning common to all theories which provides an integrative way to fine a true worldview.
c) the way you and your clients make sense of things.
d) a and c above.*
e) b and c above.

A client suffers spousal abuse and you are counseling that client. Indicate below which counselor responses are individualistic (I), systemic (S), or multicultural (M). Some responses may be of more than one orientation, in such cases select the most important dimension.

I 3. "You feel very sad and lonely right now."

S 4. "At present, your family seems to reject you and there is no place to go. Our town has no safe house for people who are abused."

M 5. "Women who are abused have real difficulty in leaving an abusive spouse. It usually takes three or more really serious cases of abuse before they can leave."

S 6. "As I hear you, you say you were abused in your family of origin as well. Tell me more about your family history."

I 7. "It takes a long time for a person to get over the hurt and sadness."

S 8. "Abuse often shows itself over the generations. What is the family history on each side?"

M 9. "Yes, abuse seems to occur not only in low socio-economic families. It is also quite common among the well-to-do."

10. The text argues that a multicultural orientation needs to take into account:

a) gender
b) race
c) affectional preference
d) all of the above *

11. Which of the following most closely represents the concept of cultural intentionality?

a) clients developing new ways of behaving, thinking, and feeling.
b) clients developing new ways of behaving, thinking, and feeling within the confines of their own culture.
c) clients developing new ways of behaving, thinking, and feeling within their own culture and other cultures as well.*
d) clients developing new ways of behaving, thinking, and feeling which represent a universal culture.

12. Cultural intentionality requires all but one of the following? Which one does not belong in this list?

a) formulating plans
b) acting on cultural possibilities
c) allowing oneself to find one's individual space *
d) reflecting on actions

13. Studies of counseling and therapy outcome have revealed all but one of the following.

a) one third of clients and patients seem to show some improvement whether or not they have formal treatment or not.
b) in general, clients who experience therapy are better off than those who do not.
c) we have fairly good ideas of which types of therapy are to be preferred over others.*
d) effectiveness of therapy seems to diminish over time.

14. "A serious moral vacuum exists because the values of a dominant culture have been imposed on a culturally different consumer." This 1982 statement by Pedersen and Marsella

a) was immediately recognized and the field of counseling and therapy started efforts toward change.
b) was largely ignored by the profession.
c) has been part of a process in which slowly we find that multicultural issues are gaining more importance in practice.*
d) needs to be modified and updated as we are now more fully aware that multicultural issues are important.

Which of the following client statements are relational and which are individualistic?

R 15. Its important to me that I'm happy, but also that my family understands what I want.
I 16. I really feel good about myself.
R 17. We have a wonderful relationship.
I 18. That really sounds wonderful to me. It makes me feel more relaxed.
I 19. "Do your own thing."

20. The core of ethical responsibility is

a) do nothing to harm the client or society.*
b) be multiculturally aware.
c) maintain confidentiality at all costs.
d) recognize your limitations.

21. Van Pelt suggests that spirituality needs to be considered more often in counseling and therapy because

a) it is no longer controversial.
b) clients are seeking a feeling of wholeness and a relationship to the transcendent.*
c) a theory of self-in-relation demands awareness of this area.
d) clients very much need the support that religion will provide.

22. The community genogram helps clients

a) see themselves in social context.
b) understand themselves in new ways.
c) find strengths from their past to use in the present.
d) a and c above.
e) all of the above.*

Essay Questions

1. Define the concept of worldview and how it relates to the Escher print relativity. Using your definition as a guideline, outline what you think if your own worldview. How was this worldview affected by your cultural surround?

2. The text stresses the importance of multicultural issues in counseling and therapy. What are the key issues in multicultural counseling and therapy in your opinion? What do you think the counseling field needs to do about them?

3. There are four building blocks of a worldview. Outline each of them and show how they are important in the therapy process.

4. Outline the three aspects of cultural intentionality with specific examples of each.

5. What is a scientist-practitioner? How might this concept relate to your own professional practice?

6. Select one of the following brief examples and outline some key ethical issues associated with it.

   a. You are working as an intern in a half-way house for troubled adolescents. You see one of the teens smoking a joint in the backyard.
   b. A student colleague in a role-playing session tells you that he or she experienced abuse as a child.
   c. A Latina/o client is referred to you. You are of a different ethnic/racial background.
   d. A European-American client tells you that he or she believes that a job was not obtained because of affirmative action.
   e. You are running a sex education class and a teen tells you that she is pregnant, but wants to keep the matter secret from her parents until she obtains an abortion.

7. How would you go about generating a community genogram for an adolescent in your home town who is having severe conflict with the family. Outline your procedures, the areas which you would encourage the adolescent to explore, and how you would draw out positives from this adolescent which he or she might draw on to work with difficult issues at home.

8. Spirituality is a topic the counseling and therapy field have tended to avoid until recently. How do you feel about the introduction of this topic in this text? What are some of the issues which argue for its inclusion? What are some issues which suggest that the topic might be better left to another department? A brief set of suggestions such as this book is only a beginning. What next steps would you suggest for yourself and the helping professions in this area?

SUGGESTED SUPPLEMENTARY READING

Integral to this book is the concept that alternative points of view regarding the counseling and therapy process are valid. The following suggested readings represent enjoyable and important background reading. All present strong statements about alternative views of the world.

Annual Review of Psychology. Palo Alto, CA: Annual Reviews, published yearly.

> Each year under varying editorship and authorship, the Annual Review summarizes current research findings in many fields of psychology. The reviews on behavior change, personality, counseling, and psychotherapy are likely to be useful background for any serious student of counseling or psychotherapy.

Gilligan, C. *In a Different Voice.* Cambridge, MA: Harvard, 1982.

> Male-oriented theory and practice may not be fully sensitive to complex sexual and cultural differences. Gilligan's highly influential work suggests a frame of reference for constructing theory from an alternative perspective.

Sue, D.W., Ivey, A., Pedersen, P. (1996) *A Theory of Multicultural Counseling and Therapy.* Pacific Grove, Ca.: Brooks/Cole

> This new book provides a new theory of MCT and would be a highly suitable second text for a counseling and therapy course which seeks to emphasize the multicultural area.

Chapter 2

The Empathic Attitude: Individual, Family, and Culture

Overview

The approach to empathy in this chapter varies from the traditional. We believe that empathic understanding which focuses only on the person is incomplete and we need to understand the individual in context of family and culture.

We believe that the empathic conditions, particularly with the cultural additions, form the basis of a helping theory in their own right. Certainly, counselors and therapists should be acquainted with these foundational skills, regardless of theoretical orientation.

The chapter discusses the following main points:

> *Empathy as a broad construct.* Here we approach empathy as it has traditionally been defined, but with the addition of multicultural considerations.
>
> *The facilitative conditions.* Here you will find an adaptation of the traditional facilitative conditions.
>
> *Empathy, family, and Rogers Issues.* This area has three purposes: 1) to help student become more in touch with their own cultural heritage, particularly as manifested in their family of origin; 2) to encourage awareness that other cultures may construct the same event differently from the culture of the helper; and 3) to introduce the important multicultural competencies which are becoming central to the definition of the effective helper.
>
> *The Multicultural Cube and the Family Genogram.* Two exercises are particularly important in helping students learn about themselves and how family and multicultural issues affect the way a client sees him or herself.
>
> *The perception check as an important skill.* Why make this a central point of the chapter? We believe that checking-out with the client and finding out how he or she reacts to the interview is a central skill to understanding the uniqueness of the client and finding out how the client uniquely constructs the meaning of the interview and our interventions.

Class Procedures

1. Images of empathy. Even though students may have read the chapter already, we find that taking them through the image exercises at the beginning is very helpful in developing trust in the class. We like to divide into groups of three or four, go through the image exercises and discuss them in small groups followed by large group debriefing. We find this experience makes empathy live for students for the remainder of the chapter.

2. The Broad Construct of Empathy. Some terms we show Carl Rogers working on videotape or film at this point. We have also used role plays in which clients are asked to make a statement and students in the group write down responses. The volunteer client then tells the student in her or his group which statements were most helpful and empathic.

3. The Facilitative Conditions.
However, especially helpful is having students rate Carl Rogers or their own role-play using the empathic rating scale or the adaptation below. We also like to have example interview transcripts available for students. They then classify the transcripts as to level of empathy shown. The instructor can then go over the tapes and discuss the specifics of rating and classification. Similar techniques can be used for each of the facilitative conditions.

Level 1—the helper's response is overtly destructive to the client.
Level 2—the response is subtly destructive
Level 3—the response detracts and/or subtracts from the client
Level 4—the response accurately hears the client and is often interchangeable with what the client said.
Level 5—the response adds something beyond the client statement
Level 6—the response significantly adds something beyond.
Level 7—the response is totally with the client and enables the client to take a markedly new perspective on the situation.

Most successful counseling will operate at Levels 4 and 5 with occasional movement to Levels 3 and 6.

We find it helpful to divide the class into groups with each group being assigned to present one of the empathic dimensions via a microskills-type presentation. Specifically, each group presents a mini-lecture on the concept to the rest of the client, does a role play in which they demonstrate the presence and absence of the concept, and then has the rest of the class practice the concept.

As part of all these presentations, it is vital that multicultural implications be constantly considered.

4. Empathy, Family, and Multicultural Issues. We have had great success in assigning homework in which the students complete their own family genogram in writing. They come to the next class with considerable interest and enthusiasm about their families of origin and themselves as cultural beings. A half-hour for sharing of important learnings they have gained for themselves from this exercise remains a highlight of the course.

We find that it is much easier to move to a multicultural frame of reference if one comes into touch with their own culture. You will often find that students of English and German descent have particular difficulty in becoming culturally aware. Students from these two (and other) cultures may say, "I have no culture." Helping them become aware that everyone has a culture is an important goal of this course.

It may be appropriate to introduce the concept of White culture at this point.

Another important point is multiculturality and biculturality. There is evidence that resistance to U.S. census categories of race and ethnicity is presently becoming more important. Encouraging your students to identity with more than one ethnic heritage may be an important contribution leading toward more understanding.

5. The Multicultural Cube. Expanding on the point in the preceding paragraph, the multicultural cube helps students become more aware of the complexity of the context in which they live. The exercise in which students examine their multiple backgrounds will be repeated again in more depth later in the course. Discussion of their unique place in the cube can be an highly enlightening experience for students.

At this stage, I like to give special attention to varying types of trauma as special cultures who need careful consideration. Most students seem to find the idea of cancer survivors, children of alcoholics, etc. as distinct cultural groupings helpful. This also seems to prepare the way for a broader understanding of the important of tolerance in racial/ethnic, gender, spiritual, and other areas.

6. Multicultural Competencies. It is important to discuss the implications of the multicultural competencies and keep these in mind throughout the course.

Multiple Choice Questions

1. The multicultural cube reminds us

    a) that racism is the central pathology of North America.
    b) that we need to work with individuals and their families if culture is to change.
    c) that each client we see likely involves some multicultural issues.*

d) that oppression of children is the most serious of all.

2. According to the text, the essence of the shift from an individualistic perspective to a family/cultural perspective requires us to

a) focus more of our attention on context.
b) eliminate individually-focused interventions.
c) add to and change present 1st, 2nd, and 3rd Force theories.
d) a and c above.*
e) all of the above.

3. Research on empathy reveals all but one of the following:

a) expert therapists of varying orientations all show empathy.
b) over the years, it has been found that Rogerian empathic therapists have the highest levels of empathy.*
c) behavioral therapists were found by Sloane to be particularly high in levels of empathy.
d) behavioral researchers have criticized the concepts of empathy.

Here is a client telling about a difficulty. Following are possible counselor responses.

Client: My spouse is drinking again. He/she came home last night reeking. I'm so upset (tears). The verbal abuse is awful.

4. Which of the following most closely represents the concepts of respect and warmth:

a) I've been there too. I had problems with abuse myself.
b) I'd like you to know that I care and believe you have the ability to work through this. *
c) Could you tell me more specifically what's going on right now?
d) At this moment I feel close to you.

5. Which of the following most closely represents the concepts of immediacy?

a) I've been there too. I had problems with abuse myself.
b) I'd like you to know that I care and believe you have the ability to work through this.
c) Could you tell me more specifically what's going on right now?
d) At this moment I feel close to you.*

6. Which of the following most closely represents the concepts of concreteness?

a) I've been there too. I had problems with abuse myself.

b) I'd like you to know that I care and believe you have the ability to work through this.
c) Could you tell me more specifically what's going on right now?*
d) At this moment I feel close to you.

7. "White" culture may be improperly named because

a) mainstream values are inappropriate for all people.
b) it covers up underlying cultural differences of people with light skin.*
c) no one really has pure white skin.
d) there is an absence of clear-cut cultural values among European-Americans and European-Canadians.

8. The text argues that the main source of our cultural values is the

a) school
b) government
c) professional psychology and counseling
d) family*

9. If you are to be empathic with others, the first step, according to the text is

a) learning about your own family and cultural background.*
b) learning about cultural differences.
c) allowing yourself to be more tolerant of differences.
d) avoiding stereotyping.

10. The perception check relates to all of these, but which defines the concept most clearly?

a) a way to learn how culturally different people have different perceptions than you.
b) learn, hear, and listen.
c) a basic listening skill of empathy.
d) listen, respond, check-out.*

11. The family chart/genogram, according to the text

a) may need to be adapted to meet the needs of each client with whom you work.*
b) is best completed using the standard traditional format as this makes it easier to compare genograms across individuals.
c) was developed to ensure that culture is considered as part of the individual interview.
d) a promising, but as yet, not fully testing strategy for individual work.

12. Experience of trauma is included within the multicultural cube. Which types of experience, according to the authors interpretation might represent trauma as culture?

a) cancer survivors, Vietnam veterans, people with HIV
b) rape and sexual harrassment survivors, families of those who have experienced trauma
c) victims of robbery and assault, children of alcoholics
d) a and c above
e) all of the above*

13. You learn through the family genogram that the client's family is distant and non-communicative.

a) enmeshed
b) conflictual
c) estranged*
d) close

14. You learn through the family genogram that the client's family is extremely close, much more so than the norm for the client's cultural background.

a) enmeshed*
b) conflictual
c) estranged
d) close

15. Considering multicultural factors, which of the following is most likely to be true?

a) estrangement of families is more likely to happen in some cultures than others.
b) what is considered closeness in one culture may be considered enmeshment in another.
c) we should encourage variations in the way we use the family chart/genogram in our individual and family work.
d) b and c above
e) all of the above*

16. The multicultural cube reminds us

a) we must first search with each client for how the issue they have relates to multicultural background.
b) in some way, most counseling and psychotherapy involve some multicultural issue.*
c) the most salient issue for many clients is culture.
d) a and c above.
e) all of the above.

17. Empathy requires, according to the text

a) individual understanding.
b) family understanding.
c) cultural understanding.
d) a and c above.
e) all of the above.*

18. The positive asset search asks us to

a) help clients become aware of their strengths and assets.*
b) positively reframe client concerns as soon as possible.
c) help clients learn to see their problems as opportunities.
d) work with clients to search for other situations which they can use more positively.

19. The Multicultural Competencies and Standards discuss spirituality and comment that we need to

a) learn a totally new set of skills for counseling and therapy.
b) reframe all client work as based in spirituality.
c) respect client religious and spiritual values and understand how these values affect expression of distress.*
d) move away from individual work so that most of what we do is in community and family.

20. It is important that you as a multicultural counselor or therapist develop

a) a keen appreciation for your own cultural history.
b) an awareness of how your own family may have shaped the way you think and behave.
c) a respect for individuality and difference and human uniqueness.
d) a and b above.
e) all of the above.*

Essay Questions

1. How would you use the multicultural cube in assessing the background of a single client? Assume that you have sufficient time to explore the many possible issues in depth.

2. Summarize the key research findings on the empathic conditions.

3. Define and provide examples of each of the following: positive regard, authenticity, and immediacy.

4. The text argues strongly that individual empathy is not enough, but that family and multicultural empathy are also important. Please summarize the text's argument and then state your own position on this critical issue.

5. The multicultural competencies are organized in three main areas: counselor awareness of cultural values and beliefs, counselor awareness of client worldview, and culturally-appropriate intervention strategies. Please define each and provide examples of how they might be useful in counseling and therapy practice.

SUGGESTED SUPPLEMENTARY READING

Carkhuff, R. *Helping and Human Relations*. Vol. I and II. New York: Holt, Rinehart & Winston, 1969 a,b.

> Two influential books on the helping process that detail the qualitative conditions. Despite their age, they are still useful and succinct presentations.

Katz, J. *White Awareness: Handbook for Anti-Racism Training.* Norman, OK: University of Oklahoma Press, 1978.

> Racism and oppression have long been a part of many cultures. This book provides a series of useful exercises for coming to terms with issues of racism and oppression. It is still widely available in bookstores.

McGoldrick, M., Pearce, J. and Giordano, J. (eds.), *Ethnicity and Family Therapy.* New York: Guilford, 1982.

> This book perhaps is destined to become a classic of crosscultural counseling literature. Presenting nineteen chapters on different ethnic/cultural groups and family patterns, it also provides solid connections with theory and suggestions for treatment. While oriented to family therapy, it will be a most useful text for those oriented to individual helping.

Rogers, C. "Empathic: An Unappreciated Way of Being," *The Counseling Psychologist,* 1975, 5 (2), 2-10.

> This represents one of Rogers' more important comments on empathy and is a succinct and lucid discussion of issues. This article is followed by a series of helpful commentaries on empathy by several authors.

Sue, D., and Sue, D. *Counseling the Culturally Different.* New York: Wiley, 1990.

The standard of the field, this book provides a theory of cross-cultural counseling and then presents specific chapters with history, suggested counseling procedures, and perspectives on counseling Asian-Americans, Blacks, Hispanics, and Native Americans.

Chapter 3

Conducting an Intentional Interview: Theory, Skills, Decisions, and Solutions

Overview

This chapter has the following overall purposes:

1. *To present constructivist and social constructivist thought which now form the theoretical framework for the microskills.* We consider the microskills to be a technology of constructivism.

2. *To summarize the microskills of attending, listening and influencing.* Here you will find the basic skills much as presented traditionally. However with each skill, the book seeks to consider multicultural issues as well.

3. *To emphasize the importance of the microskill of focus as it is central to implementing a multicultural approach to helping.* Over time we have come to an increasing realization that this once seemingly simple skill is incredibly rich. We hope this chapter presents some of the new thinking in a useful way.

4. *To present the five-stage interviewing model.* Microskills has found that a simple, decisional model can be rather readily learned and used to structure effective interviews. Moreover, this model helps students structure interviews in psychodynamic, client-centered, and other theoretical frameworks.

5. *To consider the balance sheet.* Drawing from Benjamin Franklin, the book explores Leon Mann's balance sheet as a useful tool in the helping process.

6. *To summarize solution-oriented or brief therapy as it relates to the five-stage interview structure.* We have had good results in introducing students to this method. The microskills model provides a solid grounding for these concepts. Our experience has revealed that many practicing school counselors, mental health professionals, and others find our approach most helpful.

Class Procedures

(As you might anticipate, we often use the illustrative videotapes on *Basic Attending Skills, Basic Listening Sequence, Basic Influencing Skills,* and *Solution-Oriented Counseling and Therapy* available from Microtraining Associates, Box 9641, North Amherst, MA. 01059-9641.

You will find, however, that students enjoy live instructor demonstrations and participating in classroom exercises themselves. These videos may be helpful, but they certainly are *not* essential for effective teaching of this chapter.)

1. Constructivism and Social Constructivism. Most often we simply present the key points of these ideas in lecture format. The most important idea is that we live in a world which is constructed in the mind and our "map" or constructs/ideas in our mind do not necessarily correspond to external reality.

As counselors and therapists, it is essential that we learn how to understand the varying ways our clients make sense out of the world and their personal experience. These ideas will be simple for some students, but very difficult for others. The idea that everyone does not necessarily see or experience the same thing in the same way can be troubling to those with a concrete orientation to life or those with extremely strong belief systems.

Microskills can be useful to understand that others think differently from us. A central point of this lecture is to help students see that the goal of microskills is to enter the constructed world (meaning-making system) of the client. Through using the microskills, we can learn how the client thinks, feels, and believes.

2. Attending Behavior. If this concept is new to the group, we like to use a standard exercise in which we ask a two students to volunteer to do a demonstration interview. One is the client, the other the helper. The helper's task is to do the worst interviewing job possible while the client simply tries to go on as best as he or she can. The class is directed to watch the interview and write down all they notice that is "wrong."

The interview is then debriefed and a list of inappropriate listening and nonverbal skills usually is developed. This list then can be compared to the main dimensions of attending behavior.

The next step is to review cultural differences in attending skills that modify the standard European-American practice. It is very important to note that some textbooks still teach a standard way of attending which we abandoned in the early 1970's. It seems sad that such a foundational concept is so often misinterpreted.

It is helpful to have the students practice the skills of attending in small groups in the class, or better yet, with videotape. Microskills classes that focus on practice are usually far more impactful than those emphasizing presentation of concepts.

3. The Basic Listening Sequence. Two major options are available here. The first is to have students practice each single skill using the standard microskills approach. The second is to focus on the BLS as a totality. Either way, the standard microskills approach to teaching is effective.

Introduction to skill. Define skill and its use in counseling and therapy.
Model the skill. Do a live demonstration or show a videotape of the skill in use.
Practice the skill. Divide into groups of three or four with a counselor, a client, and one or two observers who provide feedback. The client can talk about an issue while the counselor attempts to bring out the facts, feelings, and logical organization of the client's concern. Note the we focus on the counselor's ability to bring out data using the skill.
Generalization. We like to assign some type of homework in which students actually practice the skill and report back on their work.

4. Working with Children. Most counseling theory focuses on work with adults. You will find it helpful to point out to students how these same skills are used with children. Videotapes of child counseling can be helpful.

5. Influencing Skills and Strategies. Given limited time, we prefer to focus on the attending and listening skills, but the microskills teaching approach can be implemented here as well. If your group is already skilled in listening, they will prefer practicing some of the influencing skills. We particularly like to focus on the interpretation/reframe.

6. Focus and Selective Attention. The teaching of the focus skills follows the usual microskills model. Special attention needs to be given the family, "we," and multicultural/environmental foci which are less familiar in individual counseling. Our experience is that they are most effective and will be central to a developing multicultural counseling in the future.

7. Confrontation. This skill follows the same model as above. You will find the confrontation chapter in Ivey's *Developmental Strategies for Helpers: Individual, Family and Network Interventions* especially helpful to expanding the ideas presented here rather briefly. It is a central skill of the helping process.

8. Different Skill Patterns for Different Theories. A simple point is made in this section, but students feel that it gives them a comprehensive way to look at the interview—indeed, different professional helpers and different theories have very different patterns of microskill usage. Showing videotapes or films of varying master helpers and asking students to classify helping leads helps them master this idea and also give them practice in skill identification.

9. Microskills as Treatment. Clinical experience reveals that teaching skills is an effective modality for producing change, even in severely disturbed patients. You may want to examine the 1973 Ivey article which, while ancient, still summarizes clearly how microskills can be used for treatment with full awareness of contextual and even multicultural issues.

10. Decisional Style, Worldview, and Creativity. We like to begin this material with exploration of personal decisional styles. It is interesting to divide the class into groups and have them share how they go about making decisions. As you debrief the groups, note gender differences in decisional style if they appear. And, give special attention to the issue of decisions as an individual vs. a relationship matter.

Out of this discussion, the group can explore the very pragmatic worldview, still so characteristic of American society, be it individual decisions at the grassroots or even presidential decisions.

Although presented late in the chapter, we like to present varying types of creativity exercises early thus emphasizing that underlying all helping processes is the exercise of personal creativity.

11. The Five-Stage Model of the Interview. Clearly, one of the most effective classes we have is when we divided students into pairs and they work through a real decision with a classmate following the five-stage model. We find it most effective if we talk about (or better present a video or live demonstration) on each of the five stages, then give students about 3-5 minutes to work on that stage in pairs. The start and stop of such as exercise is slightly frustrating, but very effective in learning the validity of the model. (Thus, warn the students of possible frustration as you start.) Having gone through the model "start and stop," the pairs can then exchange roles this time they can work through the model without interruption.

Here is an exercise which we like to photocopy and have our students complete so that the basic model is mastered. We use it for a homework assignment in our portfolio of competencies.

Exercise in Decision Making

Ask a classmate, friend, or family to volunteer for a role-played interview in decisional counseling. Using the egalitarian model of multicultural counseling and therapy and feminist therapy, ask your "client" if you may take her or him through a systematic decisional program. You may want to outline the five stages that they will go through. For this practice session, it is usually a good idea to follow the five-stages in order, later adjusting the stages to meet individual and cultural needs. (But, if useful, certainly modify this structure in this first session.)

Good topics for your first attempt at a complete interview using this model may be: a forthcoming job search, a major purchase, a problem with a friend, colleague, or supervisor, or an issue of concern to the volunteer.

Specifically, try touse primarily listening skills and avoid advice and suggestion. You may be surprised at how well your client does with an organized decisional interview.

1. Rapport/Structuring. Some time developing rapport and telling your client about the structure of the session that will follow.

2. Data Gathering. Identification of Strengths. Define the issue or problem clearly. Use the basic listening sequence to ensure that you have brought out the major facts, the client feelings, and the organization of the issue or problem. As part of the process, spend time identifying positive assets and resources of the client.

3. Determining Outcomes. Ask the client what an ideal and *specific* solution to this problem might be. This section is often brief, but it is very important. Learn what the client's goals are.

4. Generating Alternative Solutions. "On one hand, you have defined your issue as . . . and, on the other hand, you have defined your goal as . . . . What comes to mind as a resolution?" The model confrontation and the open question following represent the essence of the approach to solutions using a decisional model. With clarity as to problem and clarity as to goal—and with a listening helper—many clients are able to generate their own new solutions.

You may wish to prompt your client to try brainstorming or raise questions, but seek not to give advice or suggestion. You may find the balance sheet helpful in organizing some complex decisions. Some clients find the balance sheet extremely helpful in complex decisions.

5. Generalization and Relapse Prevention. Make a contract with your client to implement the decision. It is tempting to let this part of the interview "slide by" (afterall, by now you and your client may be a little tired from all that thinking about the problem). It helps to make a specific agreement to follow-up with some action. Indicate that you will be in contact with your volunteer client the following week to see if something did change as a result of this interview. If the situation warrants, fill out a relapse prevention workshop as may be found in the Chapter on Cognitive-Behavioral Therapy and Counseling.

It is also important to give the students a mini-lecture pointing out that the five stages can be used to organize interviews in psychodynamic, behavioral, and other conceptions of helping.

Special attention to the model and its uses with children can be helpful.

12. Solution-Oriented Therapy and Counseling. After a brief presentation of the concepts of this system, I like to do a live demonstration. In doing so, I first share the question list and interview structure with the volunteer client. We then work our way through the list of questions together. I like to do it this way as it seems to encourage the students to work more in a mutual fashion with their clients. It also says by demonstration that having a piece of paper in front of you at the beginning may be OK so long as you work with rather than "on" the client.

Multiple Choice Questions

1. Attending behaviors, when viewed multiculturally

   a) evaporate and become meaningless.
   b) turn out to be a universal which is critical across all cultures.
   c) must be modified to recognize cultural difference.*
   d) turns out to be relevant only in a Eurocentric perspective.

2. Mirroring nonverbal behavior, says the text

   a) may help you become more in tune with your client.*
   b) is not as effective as verbal mirroring.
   c) depends on the cultural of your client.
   d) may result in dissynchonous behavior.

3. The basic listening sequence is

   a) eye contact, appropriate body language, vocal tone and verbal following.
   b) inappropriate for those culturally different from you.
   c) attending behavior and influencing skills.
   d) questions, encourages, paraphrases, reflection of feeling, and summarization.*

Identify the following counselor microskills as responses to the following client statement;

> Client: My Dad died ten years ago, but he keeps coming to mind constantly, almost obsessively. I wonder what happened? Something must have happened long ago that I forget. We had such a good relationship, he was near perfect.

4. Reflection of feeling Sounds like you cared for him a great deal.

5. Encourage Near perfect?

6. Open question Could you tell me more about that word obsessively?

7. Paraphrase Your Dad died sometime ago, but remains constantly on your mind and you'd like to understand what's going on.

8. Directive I'd like you to get an image of your father. Imagine that he is sitting in that chair across from you. Say to him what you'd like to say.

9. Self-disclosure I, too, had problems when my father passed away, but time healed things for me.

10. Interpretation/reframe Sounds to me that your feelings are very similar to those you have towards your present spouse. You seem to have need to see everyone close to you as perfect.

11. The "what" questions tends to lead to clients talking about

a) meaning
b) feelings
c) details
d) facts*

12. Listening skills with children

a) must be used carefully so as not to lead the discussion and impose your frame of reference.*
b) tend to be ineffective as children developmentally need to be told specific things to do.
c) are OK if you help them focus on causal reasoning.
d) require balance with influencing skills.

13. Provides an alternative frame of reference for the client which provides a new way of looking at old data.

a) advice/information
b) interpretation/reframe*
c) self-disclosure
d) logical consequences

What is the focus on the following statements?

14. Client You sound really happy about yourself right now.

15. Cultural/environmental/contextual That's a men's issue, so many men have concerns around power.

16. Interviewer I'm a recovering alcoholic myself.

17. Family Tell me what's going on with your family?

18. A confrontation is a useful way

a) to gain power in the interview.
b) to challenge the client in a more forceful way when it is needed.
c) to help a client see discrepancies and incongruity between words and behaviors.*
d) to change behavior directly and quickly.

19. The text indicates which theory is most likely to use a balanced focus in the interview?

a) client-centered theory
b) psychodynamic theory
c) multicultural theory*
d) all of the above
e) none of the above

20. The text indicates that interpretation is the primary influencing skill.

a) client-centered theory
b) psychodynamic theory*
c) multicultural theory
d) all of the above
e) none of the above

21. The basic listening sequence is used to help client see self-in-system.

a) client-centered theory
b) psychodynamic theory
c) multicultural theory*
d) all of the above
e) none of the above

22. Microskills are useful

a) as a treatment supplement for even seriously troubled clients.*
b) as a treatment supplement for mildly troubled clients only.
c) only as a way to train counselors and therapists.
d) b and c above.

23. With children we can expect the five stage interviewing model

a) to work pretty much as it does with adults.
b) to be almost irrelevant as children are very different.

c) to be effective at most stages, but we can expect some problems with generalization unless we use relapse prevention.
d) to be useful checklist and to help us organize our approach and thinking with each child.*

24. Solution-oriented counseling and therapy tends to use which of the following skills most frequently?

a) interpretation
b) paraphrasing
c) questions*
d) focusing

25. Native American Indian culture might appreciate some of the concepts of solution-oriented work, but one factor especially should be noted, according to LaFromboise.

a) The orientation to solution focus will not be appreciated.
b) Questioning techniques may be inappropriate.
c) The time frame of reference may be viewed differently*
d) The five stages need major modification.

26. If you woke up tomorrow and found everything resolved, how would things be? This question is a version of the

a) miracle question.*
b) a surprise intervention.
c) a culturally insensitive question.
d) a technique which solution-oriented therapists avoid.

27. Which of the five phases is most important in solution-oriented counseling and therapy?

a) rapport/structuring
b) data gathering/defining positive assets
c) determining outcomes/goal setting*
d) working on the issue/generalization

28. Constructivist thought, as presented by George Kelly, maintains that

a) our thoughts are constructed externally by culture.
b) our ideas are maintained by reinforcement by environmental contingencies.
c) we represent our environment, not merely respond to it.*
d) a and c above.
e) all of the above.

29. Social constructivist thought maintains

a) what we think is socially useful.
b) representations of experience are the individual's alone
c) representations of experience are developed in an interaction between internal and external experience.*
d) Kelly was incorrect in his formulations of constructivist thought.

30. Pragmatism is concerned with

a) what works.*
b) making therapy and counseling theory practical.
c) a linear, causal perspective on constructivist thought.
d) a practical social constructivist theoretical framework.

Essay Questions

1. Outline the five stages of the interview and the function of each stage.

2. Discuss the most important points of adapting microskill usage for work with children.

3. How can microskills we used as a treatment supplement? Develop your program for use with one of the following populations—psychiatric patients, children, or the aged.

4. Discuss the cultural variations which may appear in attending behavior.

5. Compare and contrast the microskills approach with the empathic dimensions. How might each of these concepts enrich the other?

6. Compare and constrast constructivist and social constructivist thought.

7. Discuss solution-oriented therapy and counseling (SOTC) and how it might fit into your own therapeutic framework.

SUGGESTED SUPPLEMENTARY READING

Baker, S., and T. Daniels. Integrating Research on the Microcounseling Program: A Meta-Analysis. *Journal of Counseling Psychology,* 1989, *35,* 213-222.

A comprehensive review and critique of research studies on microtraining. The review uses meta-analytic techniques and provides the best current summary of research on microskills.

Brammer, L. (1996) *The Helping Relationship.* Englewood Cliffs, N.J.: Prentice-Hall.

Brammer's small book is an excellent example of decisional counseling in action.

Evans, D., M. Hearn, M. Uhlemann and A. Ivey, *Essential Interviewing: A Programmed Approach to Effective Communication.* Monterey, CA: Brooks/Cole, 1997.

A programmed text based on microskills concepts. (Microskills emphasized in this chapter are taught in a linear programming model.) This book is an especially appropriate method to facilitate positive learning of the several skills in this chapter.

Hall, E. *The Silent Language.* New York: Fawcett, 1959.

One of the most influential books of the past 30 years in bringing us to awareness of cultural differences in communication patterns at both verbal and nonverbal levels. It is still current and available.

Ivey, A., *Intentional Interviewing and Counseling.* Pacific Grove, Ca.: Brooks/Cole, 1994.

Microskills in detail with many practice exercises. A highly useful supplement to this chapter.

Ivey, A., and J. Authier. *Microcounseling: Innovations in Interviewing, Counseling, Psychotherapy, and Psychoeducation,* 2nd ed. Springfield, IL: Thomas, 1978.

The basic research and theoretical statement underlying the concepts of this chapter are found in this book. Extensive discussion is given to analysis of the counseling and therapeutic interviews, cultural issues, and the psychoeducational approach to counseling. Includes a major review of over 175 data-based studies made of the microskills model.

Ivey, A., M. Ivey, and N. Gluckstern, *Basic Attending Skills.* N. Amherst, MA: Microtraining, 1992.

A series of videotapes and training manuals working through the basic listening sequence. Detailed instructional material for mastering the attending skills. Videotapes illustrate each skill and concept.

Ivey, A., and N. Gluckstern, *Basic Influencing Skills.* N. Amherst, MA: Microtraining, 1997.

Videotapes and training manuals on the several influencing skills. Reframing, vocational counseling, and assertiveness training are demonstrated as systematic skill sequences using microtraining approaches.

Kelly, G. (1955) *The psychology of personal constructs.* Vols. I. and II. New York: Norton.

Kelly's classic book series is where to go for the roots of constructivist thought. After 40 years, his book still reads as if it was written yesterday.

O'Hanlon, W., and Weiner-Davis, M. (1989) *In search of solutions.* New York: Norton.

I have looked at many books in this area and I find this the clearest and most useful. It would make an excellent supplement to this book if you wanted to focus on solution-oriented work in more detail.

Chapter 4

Developmental Counseling and Therapy: Integrating Individual and Family Perspectives

Overview

This chapter presents the new developmental counseling and therapy. This model provides: 1) highly specific ways to integrate developmental theory into direct counseling and clinical practice; 2) a system for integrating seemingly diverse 1st, 2nd, and 3rd Force and other theories; and 3) by extension, some practical ideas which may facilitate the practice of a multiculturally-oriented counseling and psychotherapy.

The chapter provides a discussion of the following key dimensions:

> *The DCT Post-Modern Worldview.* As an integrative metatheory, the major aim of DCT is to encourage difference and multiple perspectives. The post-modern frame focuses on different ways of making meaning in an extremely complex world.
>
> *Cognitive-developmental theoretical foundations of DCT.* DCT is a holistic reinterpretation of Piaget, but differs markedly from him with its emphasis on culture and the idea of coconstruction of knowledge. DCT is also a constructivist framework, but differs from traditional constructivism again due to the coconstructive emphasis. DCT, in truth, has much in common with George Kelly's theory of constructs. If you worked with earlier versions of this book, you likely will notice the extensions of the model.
>
> *Practical techniques of DCT.* Students will learn how to assess cognitive-developmental level in the here and now of the interview and how to match interventions to client emotional and cognitive constructions. DCT explicitly uses the network therapy model of Attneave described in the MCT chapter.
>
> *Systemic-Cognitive-Developmental Family Therapy.* Rigazio-DiGilio's formulations of DCT in family work are presented in this chapter.

Class Procedures.

1. The Gestalt Figure. This is a good metaphor for not only DCT, but also the textbook as a whole. We are concerned with multiple seeing, the ability to hold several frames of reference in mind at one time. We consider this point so important that we make an overhead of the figure and discuss its implications in some detail with the students. You may wish to use another Gestalt figure to make the same point.

As you may note, our first editions of this book focused on selecting what theory or theories each student felt most important. Research and clinical practice now leads us to believe that all these theories are relevant and it is vital that clinicians be able to work behaviorally, psychodynamically, and from a humanistic frame. Moreover, the foundational theories from this first segment of the text, we believe, will be helpful in this integration, particularly from a multicultural frame of reference.

2. Coconstruction of Knowledge and Schema Theory. We like to emphasize the knowledge and truth in counseling and therapy are constructions of reality, maps of the territory, they are not reality. Humanistic, behavioral, and psychodynamic psychology, DCT, MCT, etc. are simply constructions, useful ideas. Moreover, we believe that we learn in a multicultural context. Piaget erred in putting construction solely in the individual (although he worked from a coconstruction frame in his first book *The Thought and Language of the Child* in 1926.)

This material seems best presented around a lecture/discussion. It may be helpful to photocopy the material on assessment in this instructor guide and make it available to students. The assessment ideas there are based on coconstructive ideas and provide practical hints for construing assessment and theory in ways in which individuals, families, and multicultural systems are coordinated.

3. Identifying Cognitive-Developmental Level. This is the first and most important skill. It is the one which often provides a breakthrough for trainees in helping them understand how and why it is important to understand and match the cognitive and emotional language of the client. I like to use videotapes to present clients at the four levels (available from Microtraining Associates), but a variety of other ways are quite useful.

a. Divide students into groups and have them present examples of statements which a client might make at each level.

b. Present a stimulus such as a flower, a beautiful picture, and ask students the verbalize how they respond. You will find that students will usually present their experience at various levels and you can identify at what level the volunteer is presenting her or his issues.

c. We like to emphasize the emotional expression levels. Although DCT is usually thought of a cognitive in nature, emotion is central to change and increasingly we find that DCT's construction of emotion is useful in therapy and counseling.

4. What is Your Preferred Style of Helping? Feel free to photocopy the informal instrument "What is Your Preferred Style of Helping?" which is presented on the following pages with the Leader Guide. If you wish a larger copy and other training material, write Allen Ivey.

Developmental Counseling and Therapy

What Is Your Preferred Style of Helping?

Allen E. Ivey, University of Massachusetts, Amherst*

Purpose

This instrument is designed to help you examine your conceptual style, the way you think about relationships, and the way you make meaning in the world. It will give you some clues as to your preferred way of interacting in the counseling and therapy session. It may be helpful to you in understanding others who may approach things differently from you. Potentially, it can help you in your personal relationships as well.

Directions

1. In answering the ten questions on the following pages, focus on yourself and what is typical for you. The more spontaneous and honest you can be, the more helpful this instrument can be.

2. You'll have ten questions with four possible answers. Your task is to rank the four responses from most descriptive of you through least descriptive. You are to rank the responses from one (1) to four (4). Select the one which is most typical of you first (mark it #1), the one least typical of you next (#4), then select (2) and (3) as midpoints between the two anchors.

3. Example. Please rank the following from 1 to 4 (1 is your first choice, 4 is your last).

When I think about myself as a counselor or therapist

a. I prefer individual counseling. a.___
b. I prefer couples counseling. b.___
c. I prefer group counseling. c.___
d. I prefer family counseling. d.___

3. Move rapidly rather than worrying about your responses. *There are no correct answers or "best" way to respond.*

4. Have fun and learn a little about yourself!

Mark 1 as your preference, 4 as your last choice

1. Which type of learning situation do you prefer?
   a. Organized, structured with clear directions as to what is to be done.
   b. Highly involving and experiential.
   c. Experiences which help me apply the concepts to myself and understand myself better.
   d. Those which allow for multiple interpretations. No one right answer is really possible.

1	2	3	4
b.___	a.___	c.___	d.___

2. Emotionally, you tend to
   a. Like to look at patterns of feeling.
   b. Have specific feeling which tends to remain consistent over time.
   c. Feel deeply and immediately; feel easily in my body.
   d. Often have mixed feelings which change depending on the perspective I take.

1	2	3	4
c.___	b.___	a.___	d.___

3. Which type of counseling theories, methods, or techniques do you prefer?
   a. Rogerian and other orientations which focus on self-development.
   b. Gestalt exercises, body awareness, massage.
   c. Behavioral analysis, reality therapy, logical analysis of rational-emotive therapy, assertiveness.training.
   d. Family systems work, multicultural emphasis, examining issues of transference.

1	2	3	4
b___	c___	a___	

4. In a group counseling session, you tend to:
   a. Participate, but often like to stand back and observe the group's interaction style.
   b. Sometimes get frustrated with all that's going on. I prefer structured groups which have a specific purpose.
   c. Like groupwork which helps me understand myself and others better.
   d. Really get into it and share, I'm especially fond of here and now experiencing.

1	2	3	4
d___	b___	c.___	

5. Which describes you?
   a. Concrete
   b. Sensory-oriented
   c. Analytical
   d. Self-reflective

1	2	3	4
b___	a___	d___	c.___

Total Page 2—Do not add until finished
(The total of columns 1,2,3,4 should equal 50.)

1.___	2.___	3___	4.___

6. Stop for a moment—recall your family of origin. Allow yourself a moment of recollection before responding on the next page.

Mark 1 as your preference, 4 as your last choice

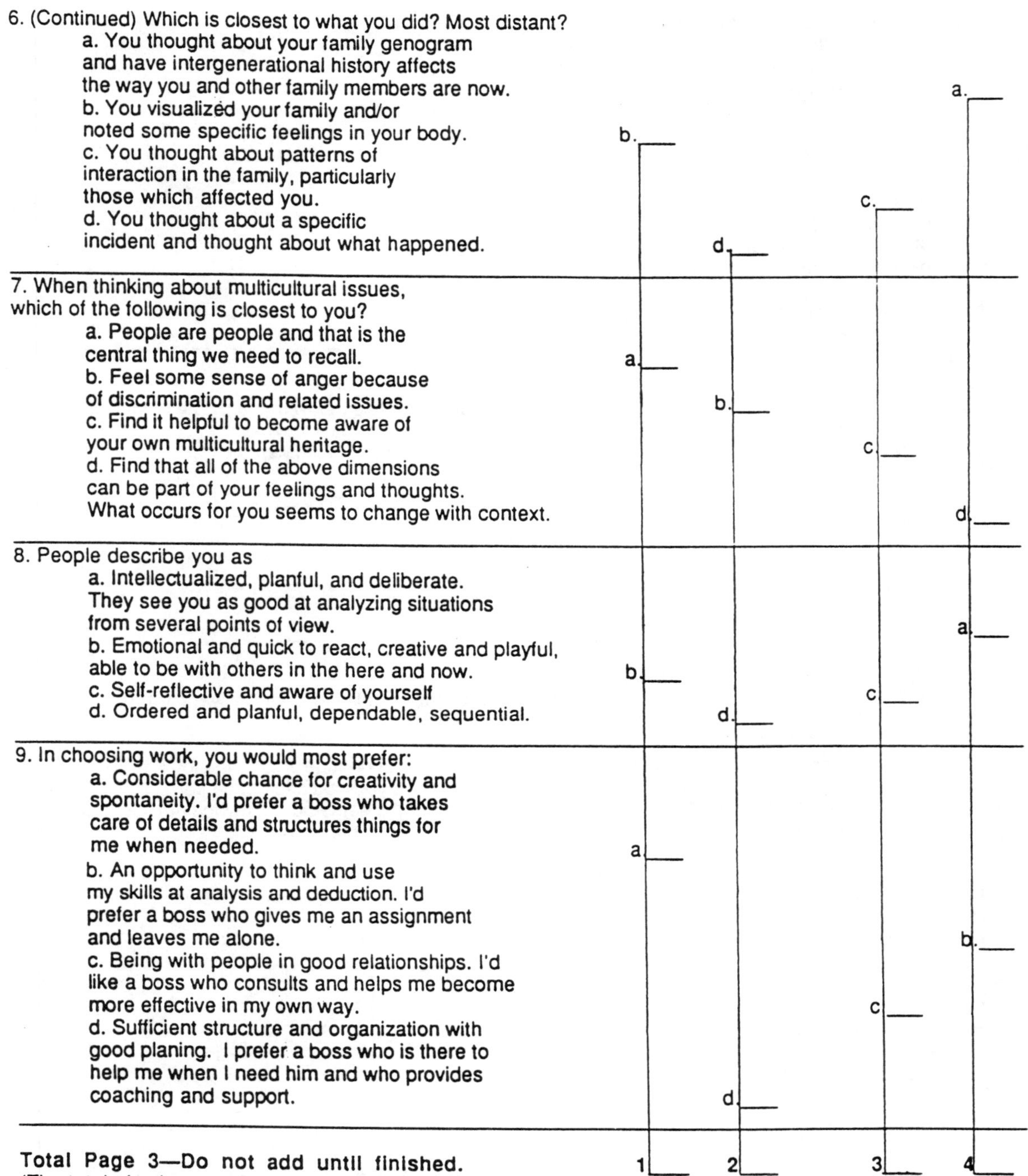

6. (Continued) Which is closest to what you did? Most distant?
   a. You thought about your family genogram and have intergenerational history affects the way you and other family members are now. — a.___
   b. You visualized your family and/or noted some specific feelings in your body. — b.___
   c. You thought about patterns of interaction in the family, particularly those which affected you. — c.___
   d. You thought about a specific incident and thought about what happened. — d.___

7. When thinking about multicultural issues, which of the following is closest to you?
   a. People are people and that is the central thing we need to recall. — a___
   b. Feel some sense of anger because of discrimination and related issues. — b.___
   c. Find it helpful to become aware of your own multicultural heritage. — c___
   d. Find that all of the above dimensions can be part of your feelings and thoughts. What occurs for you seems to change with context. — d___

8. People describe you as
   a. Intellectualized, planful, and deliberate. They see you as good at analyzing situations from several points of view. — a___
   b. Emotional and quick to react, creative and playful, able to be with others in the here and now. — b___
   c. Self-reflective and aware of yourself — c___
   d. Ordered and planful, dependable, sequential. — d.___

9. In choosing work, you would most prefer:
   a. Considerable chance for creativity and spontaneity. I'd prefer a boss who takes care of details and structures things for me when needed. — a___
   b. An opportunity to think and use my skills at analysis and deduction. I'd prefer a boss who gives me an assignment and leaves me alone. — b.___
   c. Being with people in good relationships. I'd like a boss who consults and helps me become more effective in my own way. — c___
   d. Sufficient structure and organization with good planing. I prefer a boss who is there to help me when I need him and who provides coaching and support. — d.___

Total Page 3—Do not add until finished. 1___ 2___ 3___ 4___
(The total of columns 1,2,3,4 should equal 40.)

Mark 1 as your preference, 4 as your last choice

10. When I face an important life crisis
  a. I am able to see so many points of view and possibilities that I sometimes become confused before I act. a.____
  b. I tend to react spontaneously in the moment. It just happens b.____
  c. I tend to think what the crisis means to me and my own thinking and then I do the best I can. c.____
  d. I find it helpful to think about or make a list of positives and negatives and work my way deliberately through the problem. d.____

(The total of the 4 columns for item #10. should equal 10.)

Scoring Instructions

1. Total the four columns at the bottom of each page and put your totals below in the spaces provided.

Total of Columns	1 (S/M)	2 (C)	3 (F)	4 (D/S)
Page 2	___	___	___	___
Page 3	___	___	___	___
Page 4 (above)	___	___	___	___
Column total for all 3 pages	___	___	___	___

2. Scoring Check for Accuracy of Addition
   1. If you add all four columns, the total should be 100. If the total of all your answers is 100, you have added correctly.
   2. In you do not total 100:
      a. Find the page where your error likely lies. The total of page 2 scores should be 50, page 3 should be 40, and page 4 should be 10. Did you add each page correctly?
      c. If you did add correctly, then most likely you put the same number twice or left out an answer. Change your answers that should take care of the problem.

3. Mark your scores.by points on the developmental sphere. The lowest scores indicate your preferred style areas.

4. Connect the four points and note your areas of preference. *How able are you to work with and communicate with those different from you?*

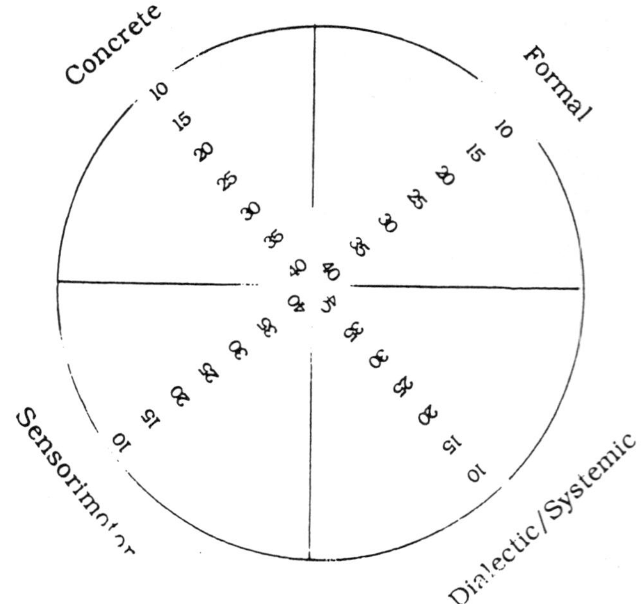

Leader Guide for "What is Your Preferred Style of Helping (by Allen Ivey)

This is an informal instrument which I use in my teaching and workshops. I've found it useful in helping students generate an understanding of the developmental counseling and therapy (DCT) framework and the way they think about the helping process. Some groups I work with are very formal and/or dialectic-systemic in their thought patterns (seems to be characteristic of counselor/therapist educators), but others are quite diverse in their patterns of response. Nothing makes a group believe in cognitive-style differences more than looking around the room and seeing that others responded differently from them.

Administration and Scoring

These are relatively simple, indicated on the form, and I find that students can take and score the instrument in from 10 to 20 minutes. The score check is particularly important and you may need to help some people find addition errors.

Theoretical Background

The developmental sphere reproduced here catches the essence of the theoretical framework. Essentially, it says that some theories of helping focus on structuring the environment for the client (eg. behavioral modification, relaxation training-body work), some on a coaching process, more concrete in orientation (eg. assertiveness training, the early stages of RET), some on formal operational consultation (Rogerian, psychodynamic theory), and some on systems of operations (feminist theory, multicultural theory, transferential issues). Furthermore, it is often important to point that that most theories do work at multiple levels. Beck's cognitive therapy, for example, while predominantly formal, does interesting work at the sensorimotor and concrete levels as well, although the dialectic/systemic type of thinking seems to be minimal.

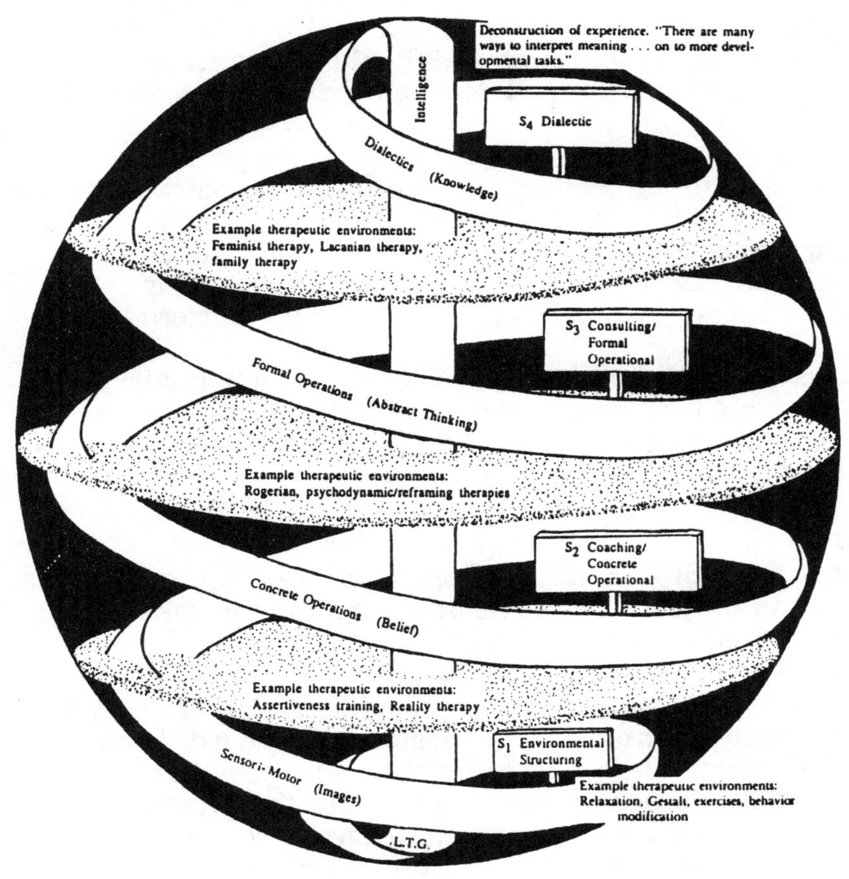

Note: This diagram was first drawn by Lois T. Grady and is used here with her permission.

Interpretation
Counseling students should be reassured that there is no right answer or best way to be. With certain clients,the sensorimotor style is best, with others, the dialectic/systemic. What is important is to be aware that we typically have a preferred style and we need to be careful not to impose our cognitive style of others. DCT stresses the importance of matching one's interventions to the cognitive-emotional style of the client.

The item stems in the instrument were designed to be positive and hopefully students will see that all of the responses are valid.

> *Sensorimotor.* Those who score most highly here are believed to be especially good at being in the moment with clients and having access to immediate experiencing.
> *Concrete.* Those who are high here tend to be good at making plans with clients, being specific, and taking action in the world.
> *Formal.* These students tend to be good at reflection and dealing. with patterns of thought of feeling. (Reflecting and experiencing feelings differ.)
> *Dialectic-systemic.* Multiperspective, these students are good at looking at systems of operations and dealing with complexity.

Each style has both strengths and weaknesses. The sensorimotor person at times may have difficulty organizing experience, the concrete person may become enmeshed in detail and have difficulty in reflecting, the formal person may be good at reflecting feelings, but have real difficulty in experiencing them fully at the sensorimotor level, and the dialectic/systemic person may get caught in thinking and have difficulties in feeling or in taking action. ***In effect, I am suggesting that full development requires us all to be more fully sensitive at each level.***

The ordering of scores is also interesting. We find a few people who have a balanced profile indicating ability to work at all levels, we find some with "spikes" who strongly prefer one style. We find those who may be predominantly formal, but also have strengths in concrete and/or sensorimotor areas. Each person appears to have a unique pattern.

The instrument seems to help students understand the DCT model and its implications at a more personal level It often helps them learn how to diagnose preferred style in their clients and start matching their intervention more carefully with client needs.

Follow-up Instruments
Style-Shift Inventory. The SSI is available from Microtraining. It presents eight cases and students develop treatment programs for the case studies. It also presents a preferred style of action score.
Gregorc Style Delineator. I really like to have my students take this instrument. It covers very good information on cognitive style, is easy to administer and score. Available from Gabriel Systems, Maynard, Mass.
Myers-Briggs Type Indicator. There are some interesting similarities and differences between the instrument enclosed here and the Myers-Briggs. On examination, I find that the sensing dimension seems to relate to sensorimotor experiences, the thinking to concrete, feeling to formal, and intuition to dialectic/systemic. Perhaps you will see something different.

Allen E. Ivey
Two Cranberry Lane
Amherst, Massachusetts 01002
(413) 253-5353 FAX (413) 549-0212

Dear Colleague,

Thanks for your interest in the instrument—*What is Your Preferred Style of Helping?* Microtraining received more requests than we anticipated, so I am writing a short leader guide to go with it. I had anticipated a fairly limited response which would come from people who are using the DCT videotapes or are quite familiar with the two developmental books.

Key references for using the instrument include the following:

Ivey, A. and Gonçalves, O. (1988) "Developmental Therapy: Integrating Developmental Processes into the Clinical Practice." *Journal of Counseling and Development, 66*, 406-412.

Ivey, A. (1988) "The Multicultural Practice of Therapy." *Journal of Social and Clinical Psychology, 5*, 1987, 195-204.

Ivey, A. (1991)*Developmental Strategies for Helpers: Individual, Family, and Network Interventions.* Pacific Grove, Ca.: Brooks/Cole

Ivey, A. (1986) *Developmental Therapy: Theory into Practice.* San Francisco: Jossey-Bass.

Ivey, A., and Ivey, M. (1990) "Assessing and Facilitating Children's Cognitive Development::Developmental Counseling and Therapy in a Case of Child Abuse." *Journal of Counseling and Development , 68*, 299-305.

Rigazio-DiGilio, S., and Ivey, A. (1990) "Developmental Therapy and Depressive Disorders." *Professional Psychology, 6*, 470-475.

Rigazio-DiGilio, S., and Ivey A. (1991) "Developmental Counseling and Therapy: A Framework for Individual and Family Treatment." *Counseling and Human Development*, 24, Vol. I.. 20pp.] (Love Publishing Company, 1777 South Bellaire Street., Denver, CO 80222.)

The articles by Ivey and Gonçalves and Ivey and Ivey above are perhaps the two best quick summaries of the developmental model. the recent article monograph published by Love extends the model to family work. For clinical work the Rigazio-DiGilio Ivey piece is most helpful.

Let me say again that the instrument is informal and in development. We'd appreciate information on the demographics of your population, scores, and you informal observations.

I find the instrument very useful in teaching and workshop settings. It helps people define themselves in relation to the cognitive-developmental processes. The instrument takes only about ten minutes and provides helpful discussion material. *It is not definitive, it is an indicator!* I see it as useful in teaching people about the developmental model. Thanks for your interest. I look forward to hearing from you with your reactions and ideas.

Cordially,

Allen E. Ivey

5. Cultural Identity Theory and DCT. These ideas could be introduced at this point or after MCT's cultural identity theory has been presented. At this point, it is often helpful to examine the similarities and differences of the two approaches. You may want to list each on newsprint or the board for your students. Then in groups, they can discuss similarities and differences. Cultural identity theory was discussed briefly in Chapter 2 and much more extensively under the ideas of MCT in Chapter 5.

How could each theoretical orientation be enriched by this process?

> First, we have noted that the language of each cultural identity level approximates the language style associated with varying DCT levels. *Developmental Strategies for Helpers: Individual, Family and Network Interventions* (Ivey, 1990) includes a chapter on this issue showing how to identify varying cognitive/emotional developmental levels using cultural identity theory.
>
> Second, DCT suggests that different strategies and theories are most effective at varying cognitive developmental levels. This is illustrated in the material on Freire in Chapter 6. It thus seems logical that awareness exercises of DCT's first level may be useful in the early stages of identity awareness, concrete techniques may be useful to clients at Jackson's third level of awareness (assertiveness, reality therapy, etc. all adapted to meet cultural differences), formal reflective techniques at the fourth level (focusing on self-in-relation or self-in-system as contrasted with a focus totally on self), and dialectic/systemic awareness and action at the final stages of cultural identity theory.
>
> Thirdly, DCT's questioning sequence offers some specific verbal interventions to facilitate expansion of awareness at each developmental level. It also suggests that certain types of perturbations and confrontations can be helpful in moving clients to new levels of awareness. We have not yet researched this issue, but clinical observations suggest that skillful use of the questioning sequence can facilitate awareness of multicultural issues, particularly self-in-system. (Also see 7 below.)

6. The Developmental Sphere. In some ways, this is early in the course of the sphere. It usually has more impact on students after they have studied other theories. At this point, we suggest mentioning it briefly and then working with it in more detail later in the course.

7. DCT Questioning Strategies. DCT's questions will be familiar to you and most students. The idea of sequencing them according to Piagetian formulations will be quite different. We have found it a powerful new tool for counselors and therapists. To our surprise, simply taking a client slowly and thoughtfully through the sequence is highly therapeutic in some cases as the client gains new perspectives on her or his situation.

Most therapy operates at the concrete and formal operational levels and the addition of sensorimotor and dialectic/systemic post formal thought and emotion seems particularly enriching to both clients and their families.

a) *Start with imaging and sensorimotor experience.* While the most simple in terms of questioning strategies, this is also the most powerful. It is important to stress ethical issues and the fact that students can "pass" if they find the experience too powerful. Sometimes, we like to do live demonstrations while other times we use videotape models. Students then practice the imaging and questions in small microskills-type practice sessions.

Often, students find themselves in tears, particularly when they image family of origin scenes. Normalize their reactions, but at the same time be available for counseling and follow-up support as well.

b) *Followup with the specific questioning sequences.* We like to photocopy the questions and have students practice them in pairs or small microskill-type groups.

c) *Return to Freire from MCT and explore how to use these questions for consciousness-raising issues.* We have found that gays who are coming out, for example, can profit from exploring their issues with a modification of the DCT sequence. Similarly, group consciousness raising for Vietnam Vets, women, or other groups can be facilitated via a similar process.

8. Generating a Treatment Plan–Focusing on depression. This material can be reviewed via lecture and students divided into groups where they combine the ideas presented here with those of Attneave in the MCT chapter. The groups then are given specific cases with the instructions to generate comprehensive treatment plans with 1) focus on individuals, their families, and other relevant groups; 2) involve multiple cognitive/emotional developmental levels.

9. Systemic Cognitive-Developmental Therapy and Family Systems. I find that students develop a more solid understanding of these ideas if they work with themselves and their own family structures. For example, does the individual come from a family which emphasizes concreteness or one which is more formal and analytical. How does the individual fit into that structure. Perhaps more powerful, however, is the practice exercise wherein students examine their own ways of constructing meaning as related to their family history. This is both a useful personal growth exercise and a solid introduction to the importance of considering family in individual counseling and therapy process.

Some other family exercises follow:

9 b. The Systemic Worldview and the Genogram. I like to have students complete a genogram before I present on family work. They like to discuss in groups their learnings as they examine their own family of origin. We then discuss the systemic and individualistic worldviews and how they might be made more compatible.

I next try to make some useful connections between family theory and individual theory. I find it most helpful to focus on the relationship between and among the following concepts. The concepts are not exactly the same, but the parallels help students see useful connections between the frameworks.

Individual language		Family language
Attached		Close
	Permeable boundaries	
Over attached		Enmeshed
	Loose boundaries	
Separated		Distant, disengaged, estranged
	Rigid boundaries	

You will also note that Kelly's constructs provide another area of communication between the two fields.

9 c. The Nature of Family. A useful exercise is to brainstorm with your group the many permutations of families (single, same sex, nuclear, etc.) and the possible cultural differences in family structures. Finally, how would these differences in family styles and cultures result in different types of individuals. *The individual's construction of reality develops in a family within a cultural context*

10. Research and DCT. We find that clients' language changes after effective counseling and therapy. Provide transcripts or watch tapes and note how client language changes over time with effective therapy. More details may be found in *Developmental Strategies for Helpers: Individual, Family and Network Interventions.*

11. Identifying One's Own Personal Style, Present Competencies, and Goals. This exercise is repeated at the end of the book in the final chapter. I find it very useful to ask students to examine where they stand in their own evolving worldview on counseling process. The exercise helps students concretize where they are and where they want to go. The final exercise in the book asks them to repeat this and can serve as a comparison point at the conclusion of the course.

Multiple Choice Questions

1. Which statement would best represent multiple seeing as defined by the text?

a) choosing the best of different theories for each client.
b) the ability to see multiple points of view.
c) holding two or more perspectives in your mind and seeing all simultaneously.*
d) generating a new theory from the best of the old.

2. DCT differs from Piaget on all but one of the following:

a) issues of cognitive development are important to adults as well as children.
b) post-formal (dialectic/systemic) thought is not necessarily more effective than sensorimotor thought.
c) schema theory is foundational.*
d) greater attention is paid of emotional development.

3. DCT argues that multicultural issues

a) are prominent in every counseling interview.*
b) need to be balanced with a wise choice of theory.
c) are so complex that we need to study them further before taking action in the interview.
d) secondary to cognitive/emotional issues.

4. The text talks about the Gloria films in which one client is interviewed by three therapists. Which observation does the book make based on the research of Meara and others?

a) Carl Rogers was the most effective therapist.
b) The client tended to take on the language patterns of each therapist.*
c) Fritz Perls was the most effective therapist.
d) The client tended to take on the language pattern of Perls, but due to Rogers client-centered orientation, she maintained more of her own constructions of language with him.

5. Coconstruction implies:

a) building a relationship which makes sense to you and the client.
b) client and counselor are influenced reciprocally.
c) reality is coconstructed between counselor and therapist.
d) a and b above.
e. all of the above.*

6. Our minds through interaction with the world build structures or theories about this world. The client develops theories about the world in relation to others, family, and culture.

a) assimilation
b) accommodation
c) schema theory*
d) DCT theory

7. In ______________ we take our constructions of knowledge and information and use them to act on the world.

a) assimilation*
b) accommodation
c) schema theory
d) DCT theory

8. In ______________ we encounter a new event or stimulus in our lives and change our older constructions of the world into new structures.

a) assimilation
b) accommodation*
c) schema theory
d) DCT theory

9. DCT theory argues that

a) clients present their problems at multiple cognitive developmental levels.*
b) clients tend to rigidly hang on to one level until therapists help them move on.
c) most clients present their issues at a disorganized sensorimotor level.
d) the most promising clients present their problems at the formal operational or dialectic/systemic level.

What is the predominant cognitive-developmental level of the following clients?

10. My family and cultural history have had a profound influence on me and the way I think about things.

a) sensorimotor
b) concrete
c) formal
d) dialectic/systemic*

11. I told my father, "What's for supper?" He said, "Why do you ask?" I said, "I'm hungry."

a) sensorimotor
b) concrete*
c) formal
d) dialectic/systemic

12. I have a pattern of difficulty with superiors. Its happened now in several jobs.

a) sensorimotor
b) concrete
c) formal*
d) dialectic/systemic

13. I can feel the pain.

a) sensorimotor*
b) concrete
c) formal
d) dialectic/systemic

Which questions would be characteristic of each developmental level?

14. What is the underlying rule in your family?

a) sensorimotor
b) concrete
c) formal
d) dialectic/systemic*

15. Could you give me a specific example?

a) sensorimotor
b) concrete*
c) formal
d) dialectic/systemic

16. What is the image that comes to mind?

a) sensorimotor*
b) concrete
c) formal
d) dialectic/systemic

17. Does this happen in other situations as well?

a) sensorimotor
b) concrete
c) formal*
d) dialectic/systemic

DCT gives special attention to emotions. Which interviewing lead relates to which type of emotions?

18. You seem to feel sad because you're going through a difficult divorce.

a) sensorimotor
b) concrete*
c) formal
d) dialectic/systemic

19. You're sad when you think of the divorce and being alone, but you're happy about your new found freedom; and, at the same time, you're feeling a bit confused about the future?

a) sensorimotor
b) concrete
c) formal
d) dialectic/systemic*

20. At this moment, you're feeling total pain.

a) sensorimotor*
b) concrete
c) formal
d) dialectic/systemic

21. You feel that sort of loneliness in many situations.

a) sensorimotor
b) concrete
c) formal*
d) dialectic/systemic

DCT argues that various theories tend to operate predominantly at varying cognitive-developmental levels (while recognizing that all theories operate at multiple levels). Which levels are predominantly represented by the following theories or techniques?

22. Gestalt hot seat

a) sensorimotor*
b) concrete
c) formal
d) dialectic/systemic

23. Client-centered examination of feelings about the self

a) sensorimotor

b) concrete
c) formal*
d) dialectic/systemic

24. Feminist theory examination of the impact of sexism on thinking and emotion.

a) sensorimotor
b) concrete
c) formal
d) dialectic/systemic*

25. Assertiveness training

a) sensorimotor
b) concrete*
c) formal
d) dialectic/systemic

26. Relaxation training

a) sensorimotor*
b) concrete
c) formal
d) dialectic/systemic

27. In generating a comprehensive treatment plan, DCT suggests

a) include therapies which represent multiple levels.
b) use network therapy to ensure that comprehensive planning is completed.
c) select the one best theory for your client and stick to it.
d) a and b above.*
e) b and c above.

28. While ethics and skillful practice are vital in all counseling and therapy, DCT suggests that it is especially important at which level?

a) sensorimotor*
b) concrete
c) formal
d) dialectic/systemic

29. Helping a client expand cognitions at their present predominant level of cognitive/emotional functioning.

a) cognitive-developmental counseling
b) emotional-developmental counseling

c) vertical development
d) horizontal development*

30. Helping a client move to a new cognitive/emotional level.

a) cognitive-developmental counseling
b) emotional-developmental counseling
c) vertical development*
d) horizontal development

31. The interactions and relationships of families functioning at primarily at this cognitive-developmental level are often guided by emotions.

a) sensorimotor families.*
b) concrete operational families.
c) formal operational families.
d) dialectic/systemic families.

32. These families recognize the powerful effect that environment has on their functioning.

a) sensorimotor families.
b) concrete operational families.
c) formal operational families.
d) dialectic/systemic families.*

33. With working with families of this type, Rigazio-DiGilio recommends a client-directed or consultative style of therapist-client relationship.

a) sensorimotor families.
b) concrete operational families.
c) formal operational families.*
d) dialectic/systemic families.

34. With working with families of this type, Rigazio-DiGilio recommends a behaviorally-oriented coaching style of therapist-client relationship.

a) sensorimotor families.
b) concrete operational families.*
c) formal operational families.
d) dialectic/systemic families.

35. With working with families of this type, Rigazio-DiGilio recommends a collaborative or mutual style of therapist-client relationship.

a) sensorimotor families.
b) concrete operational families.

c) formal operational families.
d) dialectic/systemic families.*

36. Given that African-American families are likely to be well aware of contextual issues such as racism and oppression, it would seem to be important to include some form of ____________ treatment in your work with them.

a) sensorimotor
b) concrete operational
c) formal operational
d) dialectic/systemic*

Essay Questions

1. Identify the four major levels of DCT and present example questions which the therapist could use to help clients explore these levels.

2. What are the basics of schema theory as presented in the text. How do the concepts of assimilation and accommodation work in helping clients generate new constructions of old problems?

3. How do the four levels of DCT relate to Cross's cultural identity theory? Develop a table to show comparisons? How might DCT questions be used to help clients explore issues of identity development?

4. At the dialectic/systemic level, DCT advocates that clients need to understand their issues systemically and also take action to change the system which helped bring about their problems? Discuss the positives and negatives associated with this activist orientation of DCT.

5. Discuss the issue of depression as presented by DCT. Assume you have a client who presents this syndrome. What is your treatment goal and how would you proceed?

6. Rigazio-DiGilio provides an integrative framework in which varying strategies are considered as primarily representative of sensorimotor, concrete, formal, and dialectic/systemic interventions. Present examples of family therapy strategies for each level. How might you integrate them in an overall treatment plan?

7. How could you personally use family therapy techniques in work in individual counseling and therapy?

8. Define the central issues of multiculturalism and gender in family therapy as you see them.

SUGGESTED SUPPLEMENTARY READING

Carey, J. (In Press)*Cognitive Developmental Supervision.* New York: Teachers College Press.

Carey has extended and adapted the concepts of DCT and produced a new and highly useful framework for counselor and therapist supervision.

Ivey, A. (1986). *Developmental therapy: Theory into practice.* San Francisco: Jossey-Bass.

Ivey, A. (1991). *Developmental strategies for helpers: Individual, family and network interventions.* Pacific Grove, CA: Brooks/Cole.

These two books outline developmental counseling and therapy constructs in some detail. The first book is more theoretical in orientation and provides considerable detail on concepts of assimilation, accommodation, and information processing theory. The second book is oriented to clinical and counseling practice although considerable attention is given at the conclusion of each chapter to research issues.

Ivey, A., and Ivey, M. (1990) *Developmental Counseling and Therapy.* Videotapes. North Amherst, MA: Microtraining.

This set of videotapes contains examples of varying cognitive-developmental levels, models of developmental questioning strategies, and example developmental interviews.

Haley, J. *Leaving Home: Therapy with Disturbed Young People.* New York: McGraw-Hill, 1979.

Haley has a very concrete, problem-solving orientation to family therapy. It seems allied with decisional counseling formulations.

McGoldrick, M. Pearce, J., and Giordano, J. *Ethnicity and Family Therapy.* New York: Guilford, 1982.

Students really enjoy this book with its stimulating portrayals of family structures and information from many cultures.

Chapters 5 and 6

Multicultural Counseling and Therapy: Metatheory–Taking Theory into Integrative Practice

Overview

Multicultural counseling and therapy (MCT) is conceived of as a fourth force in the field in this book. Moreover, we are presenting MCT as a way to integrate traditional theory. The following chapter on developmental counseling and therapy works nicely with MCT. Much of the technology and theory of the developmental model works well with that of MCT, particularly the theories of Freire.

Traditionally, we have taught cross-cultural counseling courses as a separate part of our curriculum. This book seeks to extend that tradition and show how we can infuse our basic training courses with a more multicultural orientation.

The concepts of this chapter are organized around Derald Wing Sue's construction of Multicultural Counseling and Therapy (MCT) as presented in D.W. Sue, A. Ivey, and P. Pedersen's (1996) *A Theory of Multicultural Counseling and Therapy.* Pacific Grove, Ca.: Brooks/Cole.

The key constructs of the chapter are defined in six major assumptions listed below They form the basis for the instructional material which follows.

I. MCT is an integrative metatheory of counseling and therapy

II. Counselor and client identities are formed within multiple levels of experience (individual, group, and universal) and contexts (individual, family, and cultural milieu). The totality of experiences and contexts is a central focus of treatment.

III. Cultural identity development is a major determinant of both counselor and client attitudes toward the self, others of the same group, others of a different group, and toward the dominant group.

IV. The effectiveness of counseling and therapy is enhanced when the counselor uses techniques, strategies, and goals consistent with the life experiences/cultural values of the client. No single helping approach or intervention strategy is equally effective across all populations and life situations.

V. The conventional roles of counseling and psychotherapy are only one of many other theoretical techniques and strategies available to the helping professional. These roles expand beyond the one-to-one therapy and involve larger social units, systems intervention, and prevention.

VI. The liberation of consciousness is a basic goal of MCT. Whereas self-actualization, discovery of the role of the past in the present, or behavior change have been traditional goals of western psychotherapy and counseling, MCT emphasizes the importance of expanding personal, family, group, and organizational consciousness of the place of self-in-relation, family-in-relation, organization-in-relation. This results in therapy which is ultimately contextual in orientation, but which draws on traditional methods of healing from many cultures at the same time.

With these two chapters, the six assumptions will be repeated and the instructional ideas around each will be presented. Overview and Class Procedures will be presented together.

A lot of material is presented that will be helpful throughout the later chapters of this book. Understanding the material here will make it possible for the student to critique traditional theory and generate new ideas for practice. *One of the purposes of this book is to enlist as many people as possible in reconsidering the field. We have a lot to do and we hope this book helps the process in some small way.*

Class Procedures

1. Reexamining the Concept of Worldview. The idea of a Eurocentric worldview as contrasted with the multicultural worldview is challenging. Students need time to find their own way to make sense of this material. I like to present the concepts of worldview, the universal and culture-specific approaches, and some of the ideas of Afrocentric theory in a brief summary lecture. Then, students divided into groups and discuss the material in their own way followed by report-outs.

Some specific questions which groups may address include the following:

1. How has the field of counseling and therapy been culturally encapsulated? What do we need to add? What still remains solid?
2. Where do you stand on the culture-specific verses universal discussion?
3. Define the main aspects of the Afrocentric worldview as contrasted with the Eurocentric. Then present other cultures' worldviews (Chinese, Japanese, Puerto Rican, Mexican, Polish, Italian, British) and contrast them with these two frames of reference.

2. Proposition I.

MCT is a metatheory of counseling and psychotherapy. It is a theory about theories, and offers an organizational framework for understanding the numerous helping approaches which humankind has developed. It recognizes that theories of counseling and psychotherapy developed in the Western world, and those indigenous helping models intrinsic to other non-Western cultures are neither inherently "right or wrong" or "good and bad". Each theory represents a different worldview.

This concept may be presented and followed by discussion. We then move to some of the specifics under the proposition.

2a. Developing New Counseling Methods and Theory. A very useful class project is developing culturally-specific theory. It is a major challenge, but I am always amazed at how well students do with it. Students can take a specific group and work through the theory generation stages outlined by Nwachuku. This can be a long-term class project and involve any number of special groups and their unique counseling and therapy needs. Students find themselves excited about developing a unique theory for women, for gay men or Lesbians, for the homeless, and for varying multicultural groups.

3. Proposition II.

Counselor and client identities are formed and embedded in multiple levels of experiences (individual, group and universal) and contexts (individual, family and cultural milieu). The totality and interrelationships of experiences and contexts need to be considered in any treatment.

3a. Focusing and MCT. A review of the microskill of focusing may be useful at this point. The focus on individual counseling is on the individual while MCT seeks to balance individual, family, and cultural perspectives.

A microskill practice exercise on this basic point may be useful. Divide the group into dyads or triads (observer for the third party). Ask them to practice drawing out a difficulty they may have had in the past which was troubling for them. Stop after about two minutes and note the focus that was originally taken—this may be problem, family, individual, multiple, or any other microskill of focus. Then spend one minute each focusing on the individual, then the family, and finally the culture. Debrief this exercise and note the difference as each area is explored.

3b. Naikan Therapy. My experience is that students find themselves almost bewildered by Naikan and the brief exercise presented here. I like to point out that many students from abroad fine themselves equally bewildered and frustrated with U.S./Canadian/Australian/New Zealand, and other Northern European approaches to helping.

I find it simply useful to present this exercise as one in which they are asked to learn a new worldview and way of thinking about therapy. You will find many object. On the other hand, you are very likely to find that those experienced with Alcoholics Anonymous do not find the concepts so strange. Helping a client see themselves in context is something traditional therapy tends to avoid—Naikan forces this issue to the forefront.

I support Naikan, but realize it is not for everyone. I like to helps students realize that a very different approach may be useful in other systems. I also find it useful at this point to listen to students objections and not try to disagree with them. This is not an easy frame of reference.

3c. Tamase and Life-span Review. The basic concepts here can be presented via lecture, but what seems to be most impactful is dividing students into groups and actually working through the exercise in developmental mapping and story telling.

I like to have students actually interview clients on their stories for each developmental stage to this point in their lives. This is a good therapeutic experience for the clients and a significant learning experience for the students. If they combine some of the DCT questioning sequence, the experience can be even more specific and powerful. But, needless to say, this must be done with full attention to ethical issues.

3d. Generating New Life-Span Theory. An extension from the above is to examine Erikson's model and consider new ways to develop more culturally-sensitive developmental theory. Students are challenged by this exercise, but soon are able to start thinking about new ways of outlining key developmental phases in life. While Erikson clearly needs respect for his important contribution, perhaps the time to move beyond his early work has come.

3e. Basic Consciousness-Raising. Groupwork is essential in MCT and one route toward helping students get in touch with themselves and how MCT relates to groups is involving them in the practice exercise here.

3f. Hansen Integrative Life-Planning Model. Hansen's model of developmental decision making focuses on the life span with an emphasis on loving, learning, labor, and leisure. Students can explore this model in considerable depth around their past and present decisions. Students particularly enjoy examining the Circle of Life as a conceptual model for some of their own major decisions. Again, completing the exercise in class is usually the best way to help the concepts "come home."

4. Proposition III.

> Cultural identity development is a major determinant of both counselor and client attitudes toward the self, attitudes toward others of the same group, attitudes toward others of a different group, and attitudes toward the dominant group. These attitudes which may be manifested in affective and behavioral dimensions are strongly influenced not only by cultural variables, but by the dynamics of a dominant-subordinate relationship among culturally different groups. The level or stage of racial/cultural identify will influence how clients and counselors define the problem, and will dictate what they believe to be appropriate counseling/therapy goals and processes.

4a. Cultural Identity Development. Again, we find it useful to involve students rather than lecture. Taking one of the cultures from the multicultural cube or, for example, Persian Gulf veterans, abused adult children, etc., students can generate their own theory of cultural identity development that will help them internalize these important concepts.

Once they have identified a theory, challenge them to present specific ideas to foster development and understanding within each stage. Then, how would they go about helping clients move to new stages?

4b. European-North American Identity Theory. Discussion and involvement with the material is important. Ponterotto's theory was generated on a rather small sample and, while it is very helpful, it is not considered definitive at this point. Students find it helpful to examine themselves from this frame of reference and to evaluate their personal growth in understanding throughout the course. Non-Northern Europeans may want to evaluate this interesting work from a new perspective.

4c. The Student's Personal Journey. Students find it helpful to complete the exercise via a homework assignment. They then can discuss some of their observations in the following class. It is often useful to repeat this exercise later in the course.

As I have gone along with this book over the years, this exercise comes to be more and more important to me and my students. It helps bring home the complexity and importance of MCT theory and practice in a very personal way.

4d. The Multicultural Cube. The cube can be again presented briefly and students encouraged to think about clients who represents more than one cultural grouping. Do the students accept the idea that language, age, trauma, etc. are valid as ideas about cultural groups?

Our experience is that students find trauma theory a useful way to extend the ideas of MCT. For example, children of alcoholic families go through stages moving from denial to acceptance and perhaps transcendence. These stages of trauma and grief closely parallel the ideas of MCT's cultural identity theory.

5. Proposition IV.

> Counseling and therapy's effectiveness is enhanced when the counselor uses techniques, strategies, and goals consistent with the life experiences/cultural values of the client. No single helping approach or intervention strategy is equally effective across all populations and life situations. The ultimate goal of multicultural counselor/therapist training is to expand the repertoire of helping responses available to the professional, regardless of theoretical orientation.

5a. The Practice of Multicultural Counseling and Therapy. We have an expanding theory about MCT, but relatively limited written material, particularly in textbooks, about "what to do." It may be useful to attempt some role-plays and to take a more clinical emphasis to help students realize that MCT can be practiced and does have a distinct and unique role. The transcript attached here on feminist theory will be very helpful in this regard.

5b. Internal and External Locus of Control. We find it helpful to have students work in practice microskills-type role-plays around this issue. We divide the class into groups and ask the role-played client to portray him or herself as having been discriminated against as part of one of the classifications of the multicultural cube. In the first role-play the counselor can focus on individualistic "I-statements" and in the second on the situation and "cultural/environmental/contextual" issues. The distinction and the importance of balancing internal and external locus of control issues becomes apparent. Discussion usually follows on the responsibility of the counselor/therapist to take action in an often racist/sexist world.

5c. Feminist therapy. Students enjoy discussing the major aspects of feminist therapy and contrasting these ideas with much of traditional theory. Discussion of these ideas in small groups is helpful—but ensure that each group examines traditional theoretical approaches and how they might be validly and helpfully used with women. Feminist theory is not opposed to traditional theory; rather, it seeks to find a new and more useful integration.

Following is a transcript of a feminist therapy interview which has been edited for brevity and clarity. You may want to copy this session for your class or workshop and discuss it in some detail as to how it is similar and how it is different from traditional modes of helping.

This brief summary of feminist therapy illustrates that a clearly articulated alternative approach to counseling and therapy is evolving. The following typescript from an interview conducted by Mary Ballou illustrates some of the issues and the therapeutic approach that one might find in this orientation. You will note that the method here is quite different from other theories to helping. Particularly, consider the mutual exploration of both therapist and client and the manner in which Ballou focuses on cultural/environmental issues. The following excerpt is also interesting as it illustrates how the egalitarian relationship leads toward discovery of self-in-relation. This interview is used with Dr. Ballou's permission.

Counselor: In our first meeting last session you gave me information about your history, current life, focus of concerns and your worldview. We clarified your feminist values orientation and your wish to explore your career/family conflicts as well as the options open to you and your perceptions and feelings about them. I shared with you some information about my orientation to counseling and my feminist worldviews. We also agreed to work together for six sessions and then reevaluate. I am wondering what kind of reactions you have had to our first session and in the intervening time?

Client: Well, there, my reactions are complex and many. I felt easy with you and your explanation of why you needed particular information or why you were suggesting certain things, like the contract, made sense and I relaxed. It was easy to tell you of my history, development, and current confusion. I felt relief that you did not see me as sick or incompetent. It helped when you suggested that many women face similar issues and can resolve them and in different ways. I felt supported, understood, and not trivialized as I often have when I have raised these issues before. Also I felt hopeful that I was not alone but at the same time the options would be mine, not standard sexist or feminist ideology about what women should do.

Counselor: Those reactions are certainly complex and well thought out as well as positive. Were there any other reactions that were less clear or troublesome?

Client: There's one but it is a bit vague. It's, well, I don't know, aha, well, how to think about our interaction. This is not like the counseling I had years ago which was more removed and professionally distant, but it is not like my friends in the feminist support group either.

Counselor: Is there a context or relationship that it is similar to for you?

Client: Perhaps it is like my colleagues with whom I do joint work in the research grant, but in our sessions there seems more room for me and my needs. And it is sort of like the feelings I had with the Licensed Nurse practitioner who worked with me in the home-birth of my last child, but not so focused. But there really is no other model which fits this experience very closely.

Counselor: So our interaction does not fit with your past experiences very well. How is that for you?

Client: Well, I am unsure about how to relate with you. Like do I invite you to lunch, ask personal questions, or treat you like an expert or boss?

Counselor: So the role and boundaries are unclear and, am I right, unsettling?

Client: Yes, yes to both, and I am sort of anxious about it.

Counselor: It is a bit difficult to feel comfortable in an interaction when the roles, boundaries, and expectations are undetermined, unknown, and unexplored. It is similar to being in a new territory. We can talk about our relationship and its boundaries now if that would be useful to you.

Client: Yes. I think it would be.

Counselor: O.K. we will do that--but first I would like to focus on our process for a moment because I think it relates to your general issues in the career/marriage conflicts. I wonder if you would have volunteered this discomfort in our relationship if I had not asked again about your reactions after you told me the positive and clear ones? I also wonder if withholding confusion and/or personal discomfort in relation to others is a pattern for you.

Client: That observation is very accurate, withholding my own discomfort and meeting others' needs in the family and requests on the job are patterns of mine.

Counselor: So our interaction here has just reproduced your general characteristics of giving others' feelings, needs, requests more importance than yourself. What are your thoughts and feelings about that?

Client: It embarrasses me, I don't think I should do that but it is such a habit. Also I guess it angers me its such a self-defeating pattern. I seem to do it naturally.

Counselor: Do you see any connection with this pattern and women's sex role ascribed behavior?

Client: I feel an intuitive rightness but have not made a sex-role linkage. Sexist conditioning would of course affect communication patterns.

Counselor: It is an important point and one we might want to pursue more fully. The novel *A Room of One's Own* illustrates the issues quite well. Perhaps you might read the book and then we can discuss your reactions and any possible relevance to your life. But I interrupted before. Should we now pursue this or return to discussing our relationship, boundaries and expectations? (Mary Ballou, 1984, Northeastern University, by permission.)

5d. Applying Feminist Theory in Practice. The practice exercise in the chapter will be useful in "bringing home" the concepts of the theory. Gender analysis is particularly important and really helps both sexes begin to see how they can use the ideas of this model.

5e. Panigua and Counseling Culturally Different Clients. My experience is that his ideas are controversial with students. I like his forthright approach which demands awareness and change. But my students comment that it is more complex than his suggestions.

In one recent course, his opinions became the central issue of the course and were debated throughout. This was a profitable and challenging exercise for all (including me!).

Thus, I like to engage in active discussions in large or small groups around such issues as:

Is Paniagua right? Are these specifics usable?
How would you change them?
Would you prefer to have no suggestions and just work with each "unique client?"
What value is a list of cultural suggestions such as that presented by Paniagua.

6. Proposition V.

MCT stresses the importance of multiple helping roles developed by many culturally different groups and societies. The conventional roles of counseling and psychotherapy are only one of many other theoretical techniques and strategies available to the helping professional. These roles expand beyond the one-to-one therapy and involve larger social units, systems intervention, and prevention.

6a. Family Therapy with African-American Families and Network Therapy. I like to give special attention to this material. The orientation of Attneave and Cheatham is quite different from other family therapists with the stress on network and action in society. Minuchin knew Attneave in the late 1960's at the Philadelphia Child Guidance Clinic, but tended to ignore her work in subsequent years. Recently, in the *Family Networker* he finally indicated that work with poor families must involve community action if their problems are to be solved. Unfortunately, he did not cite his colleague, Attneave, although she was thirty years ahead of him in awareness on this issue.

6b. Network therapy. Implicit in the Attneave network model presented here is case management, something which counselors and therapists often tend to avoid. It is our very avoidance of integrated case management that is one of our major problems in reaching non European-American clients. Furthermore, you will find that the network approach and MCT can benefit European-Americans just as much as other cultures.

Students will need some time to process the concepts of network therapy. Traditional theory seems to operate under the "Lone Ranger" theory of helping (i.e. one person can do it all alone) and network theory is clearly a different approach. A lecture plus some small group time seems important.

To help understand the concepts of network theory, it will be helpful to summarize the adaptation of network intervention with children. Students in groups can then apply the same approach to other clinical populations such as teen-age drug abusers, adult alcoholics, and families with an acting-out or bulimic child.

6c. The Family Rule Exercise. This is another exercise that works well as homework or as an in-class experiential session.

6d. Traditional Healing. Students seem to find this material quite fascinating, particularly the idea that traditional healing methods follow a similar structure to that of present-day psychotherapy and counseling. This section is not designed to make the expert in this area clear, but to start a process of respect for cultural difference and approaches which are markedly different from our mainstream.

Christie Achebe who was so helpful to us in making these connections is married to the prize-winning author, Achebe, whose *Things Fall Apart* is a classic of African literature. This book would make an excellent supplementary reading for any multicultural course.

It is also important to keep in touch with Courtland Lee's latest writings in this area. See, for example, his chapter in Sue, Ivey, and Pedersen's *A Multicultural Theory of Counseling and Therapy.*

7. Proposition VI.

> The liberation of consciousness is a basic goal of MCT. Whereas self-actualization, discovery of the role of the past in the present, or behavior change have been traditional goals of western psychotherapy and counseling, MCT emphasizes the importance of expanding personal, family, group, and organizational consciousness of the place of self-in-relation, family-in-relation, organization-in-relation. This results in therapy which is ultimately contextual in orientation, but which draws on traditional methods of healing from many cultures at the same time.

7a. Freire and Liberation of Consciousness. This is a concept-dense section which integrates past material and extends the ideas into new arenas. Most particularly, it suggests that counseling and therapy may be viewed as consciousness raising of self-in-context—present social context, family and historical context, cultural context. Implicit in this section is that therapy which does not consider the cultural, the situation, and the unique developmental history of the client is incomplete.

What this adaptation and interpretation of Freire suggests is that most and perhaps all of our clients go through identifiable cognitive/emotional stages/levels which parallel cultural identity development theory. The model also provides a way to integrate traditional helping theory at varying stages of development.

A full hour or more is need to cover this material adequately. I find it important to cover the material in lecture and to go through the case presentation in some detail.

Then, I like to divide students into groups asking them to consider cases who have suffered varying types of trauma. The group's task is to identify the developmental stages that clients might go through on the way awareness of self-in-context (the client moves form an embedded self-blaming consciousness to awareness of self-in-system). Specific attention should be paid to expanding awareness of the client at each stage.

7b. Practice Exercise with Freire. The practice exercise works well and will help students seek how to help clients see themselves in cultural and social context. Many of my students find the exercise basic to their understanding and using MCT.

Multiple Choice Questions

1. Donald Cheek in 1976 challenged the field of counseling and therapy stating:

a) I am advocating treating one segment of our population quite differently from another.
b) African-Americans do not respond from many therapeutic approaches to which Whites respond.
c) The cognitive-behavioral frame of reference is irrelevant to African-Americans.
d) a and b above. *
e) b and c above.

Which of the following statements is characteristic of the universal approach to multicultural counseling (U) and which are associated with the focused culture-specific approach (F)?

2. U Defines culture broadly including age, gender as well as race/ethnicity.

3. F Emphasizes issues of race and ethnicity.

4. F Given the history of racism, we need to focus on that issue primarily.

5. U Emphasizes the importance of language as the vehicle of counseling and therapy.

6. The text traces the origins of MCT to

a) the Black consciousness-raising movement of the 1960's.*
b) the feminist consciousness-raising movement.
c) the Gay Pride movement.
d) all of the above.

The Afrocentric (A) and Eurocentric (E) worldviews may be characterized as:

7. A Holistic.

8. E Focusing on the individual.

9. A. Interdependent

10. A Focusing on collective survival

11. E Identifies discreet and knowable parts.

12. A harmonious blending and cooperation.

13. E Emphasizes competition.

Cross identifies five levels of cultural identity developmental theory which the text has worded as follows: 1) Naiveté, 2) Encounter, 3) Naming, 4) Reflection on self as a cultural being, 5) Multiperspective internalization. The text indicates that this theory also relates to women's identity theory, and Vietnam Veterans. Also, by extension, you can expect these levels among other types of multicultural populations. Indicate the level of identity development below in the following examples.

14. 1 (A European-American) "The color of one's skin doesn't make a difference."

15. 3 (Vietnam Veteran) "I'm really angry about the way the U.S. ignored us when we got home and still fails to recognize us for what we did."

16. 4 (African-American) "I'm tired of fighting racism. I just want to be with my people and get my own act together."

17. 5 (Woman) "Sexism is a terrible thing. It has really hurt women and I've suffered personally and many times I've been angry. But, at the same time, I know there are men who are involved in the struggle and I welcome their help. Each of us is different and somehow the same."

18. 2 (Cambodian-American) "I just need to try harder. People will accept me if I learn better English and more North American ways."

20. "What happens next depends on what my extended family thinks I should do." This might be an example of

a) internal locus of control and relational thinking.
b) external locus of control and relational thinking.*
c) internal locus of control and autonomous thinking.
d) external locus of control and autonomous thinking.

21. All but one of the following are true about research on ethnic minorities.

a) Minorities are more likely to think of psychological difficulties as organic in nature.
b) Majority counselors tend to reflect racial stereotypes held by their culture.
c) Minority clients can only be seen by minority counselors.*
d) Acculturation of the counselor may be more important than racial/ethnic identification in terms of how the client accepts them.

22. Feminist therapy may be identified by all but one of the following.

a) egalitarian relationship.
b) use of community resources.
c) a quiet, but effective counseling style.*
d) information giving.
e) uses traditional theory with awareness of multicultural issues.

23. *Conscientizacào* may best be defined as:

a) liberating clients from self-blame and helping them see themselves in relationships to others and their culture.*
b) liberating clients from unneeded anger and helping them see themselves in relationships to others and their culture.
c) liberating clients from self-blame and helping them see how individual action can lead to growth and human development.
d) liberating clients from unneeded anger and helping them see how individual action can lead to growth and human development.

24. Traditional healing, according to the authors

a) has much in common structurally with western psychotherapy and counseling.*
b) has many excellent strategies which need to be used as soon as possible by the field.
c) has a limited place, even in traditional societies.
d) must be considered in the realm of mystery is to be avoided.

25. MCT, using Freire's *conscientizacào* maintains

a) that we can match our helping interventions to the varying cognitive and emotional levels of the client and in this way help them find their own critical consciousness.*
b) that each of us must eradicate racism and sexism from society.
c) a general approach to helping can be developed, but it must come from a multicultural context.
d) all of the above.

26. Attneave's network therapy focused on

a) individual counseling which helped clients see themselves in context.
b) family counseling which emphasized the context of the family.
c) group counseling which helped individuals see themselves in relation to the group.
d) the important network of relationships including nuclear family, extended family, the neighborhood, and community.*

27. Network interventions can be adapted for work with children by

a) bringing children together in groups.

b) helping the teacher understand the child.
c) bringing together larger groups of helping professional and family members.
c) b and c above.
d) all of the above.*

28. Hansen's' Integrative Life Planning Model

a) emphasizes the importance of making decisions in as logical a fashion as possible.
b) stresses relapse prevention.
c) emphasizes that decisions are intuitive in nature and require creativity.
d) stresses that we make decisions in relationship to others.*

29. The circle of decision making as it relates to the five-stage interviewing model emphasizes

a) the importance of clear linear decisions.
b) that we need to follow the five-stage model as we learn other theories of helping.
c) that ordering information is critical for success.
d) that we must adapt the five stages to meet the unique individual and cultural background of the individual.*

30. Nwachuku describes the relational patterns of the Nigerian Igbo as

a) emphasizing the extended family as decision makers for the individual.*
b) emphasizing individual decisions.
c) emphasizing nuclear family decisions.
d) all of the above.

31. The Nigerian Igbo are not Africa-Americans or African-Canadians. Therefore the text emphasizes that

a) the methodology of studying an African culture has little relevance for the helping process in North America.
b) we can use a model for studying culture and learn to develop culturally-appropriate helping theories.*
c) we must acknowledge cultural difference wherever we find it.
d) what we learn in Africa can be applied directly to North America with minor modification.

32. Tamase's theory of life-span development differs from Erikson in that

a) the focus is on accountability for developmental change.

b) Erikson's theory is noted as less culturally sensitive than is generally believed in the field.*
c) it is based on more research.
d) it is less complete and pays less attention to cultural difference.

33. Consciousness-raising, according to the text is

a) something that only highly skilled therapists should approach.
b) useful in helping clients raise their self-understanding.
c) a rather simple technique which all should be able to use easily.
d) an important group strategy within MCT theory.*

34. Cheatham argues that family therapy with African-American families

a) is not possible given the past Eurocentric history of family therapy.
b) is most effective using Attneave's network approach.
c) must recognize and negotiate issues of power between the family and therapist.*
d) must include consciousness-raising using cultural identity theory.

35. "Should race and ethnicity be discussed as part of the family therapy process?" Cheatham recommends

a) no, as it can be damaging to the therapist-family relationship.
b) yes, particularly if the therapist is not of a similar racial/ethnic background.*
c) it depends on the educational and experience of the therapist.
d) it depends on the cultural identity level of the family.

36. Naikan therapy is likely to be controversial as a method in U.S. and Canadian societies because

a) it seeks to open old issues which are best forgotten.
b) it is antithetical to the ideas of Alcoholics Anonymous.
c) it asks one to focus solely on how one feels about the self.
d) it focuses on harmony as opposed to self-actualization.*

Essay Questions

1. Compare and contrast the universal approach as presented by Fukuyama with the focused culture-specific approach as presented by Locke. What is your position on this important issue?

2. Outline the five key stages of cultural identity theory as presented by Cross and provide an example of each.

3. Generate a new theory of identity development which might be used for gay men or Lesbians, the aged, or the physically challenged. Give an example of each.

4. Define the multicultural cube and how it might be used to help counselors understand the psychotherapy and counseling process.

5. Define feminist theory and its major contributions to the profession. How can it be used to integrate other theoretical approaches to helping?

6. Define *conscientizacào* and indicate how it might be used in a psychotherapy of liberation with a Vietnam or Persian Gulf Veteran. Provide specific examples of interventions at varying stages.

7. How would you use Attneave's network therapy in an ideal sense if you were working with a teen-age alcoholic?

8. Compare and contrast traditional healing with the North American and European systems of helping.

9. How could you use consciousness-raising strategies as part of your helping system?

SUGGESTED SUPPLEMENTARY READING

Asante, M. *The Afrocentric Idea.* Philadelphia: Temple University Press, 1987.

> This book is considered the centerpiece of Afrocentric scholarship. More than any other single book, it demonstrates the content and context, meaning, implications of the Afrocentric frame.

Ballou, M., and Gabalac, N. *A Feminist Position on Mental Health.* Springfield, IL: Thomas, 1984.

Chaplin, J. *Feminist Counselling in Action.* London: Sage, 1988.

> These two books outline a very pragmatic and useful description of feminist counseling and therapy. Students, both women and men, enjoy these books and appreciate their clarity and utility.

Pedersen, P., & Ivey, A. (1993) *Culture-Centered Counseling.* New York: Greenwood.

> Specifics of working with many multicultural situations. Focuses on model cultures and provides many exercises useful in coordination with this book.

Ponterotto, J., and Casas, M. *Handbook of Racial/Ethnic Minority Counseling Research.* Springfield, Il: Thomas, 1991.

A useful summary of multicultural research to date with a description of necessary next steps.

Sue, D.W., Ivey, A., and Pedersen, P. (1996) *A Theory of Multicultural Counseling and Therapy.* Boston: Allyn & Bacon.

Detailed presentations of the six propositions of this chapter followed by highly useful evaluations and commentaries by leaders the MCT movement.

Wilson, J. *Trauma, Transformation, and Healing. : An Integrative Approach to Theory, Research, and Post-Traumatic Therapy.* New York: Brunner/Mazel, 1989.

Trauma, this chapter argues, is a culture in itself. This book represents an excellent theoretical/practical approach to trauma. The primary focus is on Vietnam, but the principles of coping with trauma go far beyond post-traumatic stress disorder.

Thanks to the scholarship and precision of such individuals as Wilson, it is now recognized that psychic trauma, similar to that experienced in Vietnam, exists among individuals who have experienced child abuse and incest and the repeated injustices of racism, sexism, and homophobia. This book gives its primary attention to Vietnam, but you will find that its scholarship and utility form a useful background for any type of trauma practice.

Chapter 7

Psychodynamic Counseling and Therapy: Part I: Conception and Theory

Overview

Psychodynamic thought is presented in this chapter in ways which are quite different from traditional texts. While still based on traditional theory, the emphasis here is very much on attachment theory and using psychodynamic theory in a culturally-relevant fashion. It is our belief that this much-maligned theory has considerable value for all therapists, regardless of theoretical orientation.

But, to be meaningful requires that we move away from traditional concepts to the well-researched perspectives of John Bowlby. Moreover, ideas from developmental counseling and therapy around personality style/disorder helps students ground the concepts in a practical way.

Chapter 8 of this Instructor Guide presents a case study "The Fire Tower" which you may wish to photocopy and make available for your students as they consider the ideas of Chapter 7.

My students start the chapters resistant to this approach due to its history of sexism and classism. As they learn the more modern approaches suggested by Bowlby and Taub-Bynum, they become more interested in psychodynamic thinking. They discover that case conception benefits from understanding these constructs and that the theory can be used readily in concert with client-centered and cognitive-behavioral frames of reference. I also find that students understand the cognitive work of Aaron Beck more fully if they have first mastered the concepts of this chapter. Beck originally worked psychoanalytically and much of his cognitive methodology still resembles psychodynamic techniques. (Needless to say, my conversations with Beck's staff suggest some disagreement with these statements, but Beck's use of images, tying present behavior to past learned behavior, is very consonant with the psychodynamic frame of reference presented here.)

You may even want to present these two chapters to your students as a psychodynamically-oriented CBT. You will find that the DCT perspectives on personality style/disorder quite complimentary to those of Beck.

The key constructs of this chapter are defined as follows in the early pages of the chapter and are repeated here as these six points are foundational for this and the following chapter:

1. Client developmental history is important and needs to be considered for full client understanding. Freud is often considered the first developmental psychologist. Basic to his orientation and the psychodynamic frame of reference is the importance of childhood experience in determining how we act and behave in the present.

2. Important in our developmental history are the key people we have related with over time—our object relations. In psychodynamic language *object relations* is the term given to relationships with people and important objects in our life. We develop in relationship to people—our family, friends, and peers. In addition, multicultural factors influence the course of this developmental history.

3. We are unaware (unconscious) of the impact of both biological needs, the impact of past developmental object relations on our present behavior, and of cultural determinants. The unconscious is the reservoir of our memories and biological drives, most of which we are unaware.

4. We constantly act out in daily lives our developmental history and our unconscious biological drives. From the psychodynamic frame of reference, we are heavily ruled, sometimes even completely determined, by forces outside our awareness. However, some theories claim biology is central in unconscious development while others focus more on life-span developmental issues. And—increasingly the influence of multicultural factors in unconscious development is being recognized.

5. The task of counseling and therapy is to help the client discover the unconscious roots of present behavior. Through psychodynamic techniques and concepts such as free association, interpretation, and analysis of transference, we can help the client discover and understand the background of present behavior, thoughts, and feelings.

6 Personality Style/Disorder. How to use psychodynamic theory for case conceptualization. DCT's model of case analysis is presented. This model is closely related to the constructs of John Bowlby.

Beyond these underlying constructs, many underlying and hopefully more culturally relevant ideas are presented throughout this chapter. Again, I'd like to stress the importance of the above six ideas for *understanding* what is happening with the client. An understanding of the client from this frame, I believe, will help therapists work more effectively from cognitive and other modes of counseling and therapy.

Class Procedures

1. Imaging and The Major Premises of the Chapter. I like to begin this chapter by asking students to close their eyes and think of a current problem or issue in their current life. I ask them to image the problem (using DCT sensorimotor-type questions—what do you see, hear, feel) and to focus on it. Then I ask them to locate the feeling in their body and to free associate to whatever occurs to them in their developmental history. Again, I ask them to get an image in their mind from the past. Then, I ask them to meditate on the two images and discover how they might relate. How are the two connected? What is the meaning?

I then ask students *who feel willing to share* to discuss their experiences with another person or in a small group. Those who may not wish to share are asked to write their observations in a journal. I then cover the five points above and students usually provide examples from this brief exercise to help make the five major points more clear.

2. Multicultural Issues and the Psychodynamic Tradition. I find it helpful to ask students to share their thoughts about this theory and gender and multicultural issues in small groups. We then report out and honestly discuss some of the matters around this theory which have occurred over time. I like to stress that it is vital to keep their individual critiques and the cultural critiques at the beginning of the chapter in mind as they read and work through the two chapters.

3. Central Constructs of Psychodynamic Theory. This material can be presented in lecture form or a variety of more experiential presentations may be made. Following are a few ideas:

3.1 Id, ego, superego. As I stress object relations theory, particularly from an environmental frame of reference, I like to focus on the superego and how we learn to internalize societal, cultural, and family roles. It is helpful to divide students into groups and there they can discuss the way homophobia, discrimination against the disabled, or Vietnam veterans leads to an internalized superego which is self-defeating.

If you prefer to work from an ego psychology ("strengthen the ego") frame of reference, these same issues may be discussed from a psychoeducational frame. Adler and Anna Freud, for example, were interested in teaching clients skills as a way to increase their ego functioning.

3.2 Ego defense mechanisms. Often this material is presented mechanically with minimal attention given to *how the defense mechanism arose.* Students actually begin to use defense mechanism theory when they understand that the defense mechanism was developed as a positive way to deal with often insane situations. Of course, now the defense mechanism works against the client. The psychodynamic task is to respect and value the defense mechanism, unravel its developmental history (and for this attachment theory is most helpful), and then perhaps move to cognitive-behavioral and other methods to help change old ineffective cognitions and emotions.

I like to give some attention to Bowlby's important work and then ask students in small groups to consider how various types of personality styles or problems might have developed over time as originally as functional adaptations.

3.3 Developmental Roots of Present Behavior and Thought. Here the traditional oral, anal, and oedipal issues are discussed, but within the functional model of trust, control, and sex-role development. If you have time, it is helpful to students to learn more about the controversy's around the Oedipal period. I sometimes like to have a feminist theorist in to critique Freud's traditional position.

Multiculturally, it is important to note that Freud's construction of correct developmental progressions came out of 19th century Vienna. What is useful developmentally in one culture may be pathological in the next.

3.4 What is a caregiver? Object Relations and Repeating Patterns of Behavior. It is very important to note that the notion of caregiver varies from culture to culture. This point is central to understanding difference and to making psychodynamic thought culturally relevant. The idea that the caregiver can be more than one person is vital to breaking out of the traditional psychodynamic straitjacket.

3.5 John Bowlby and Developmental Ecology. Bowlby and Ainsworth's work has become increasingly recognized—the American Psychological Association gave them a major award recently. Bowlby's concepts are not speculation—they are founded on a solid base of research. It is beginning to appear that there is more empirical research on Bowlby's work than all other psychodynamic models together. For survival in the world of the future, some knowledge and skill in Bowlby's ideas seem essential.

The most important points of Bowlby's theories focus on the child's reaction to separation (both in the original observations in World War II and the more recent empirical research of Mary Ainsworth). Students should be able to identify the patterns of secure attachment, anxious-ambivalent attachment, and the avoidant pattern.

3.6 The Family Unconscious and a Multicultural Psychodynamic Theory. More than anyone else, Taub-Bynum has helped make psychodynamic theory culturally relevant to me. The idea that we learn our patterns of attachment, our defense mechanisms, and our patterns of ego and super-ego functioning in our families of origin is one of those simple, yet profound observations that can make such a difference in the field.

A useful exercise is to have students develop a family genogram with a focus on family style over the generations. Students from a Swedish background begin to understand that they indeed have a different cultural history from those of German background. Haitians and Southern African-Americans learn to understand how they are personal bearers of the culture.

I like to use microskills-type practice sessions around Taub-Bynum's ideas. In effect, I ask students to interview each other using the basic listening sequence to draw out family stories and themes. Then, by focusing on the individual, the family, and the cultural context, students in the class learn to look at themselves in some very new and some very exciting ways.

The dream exercises in Chapter 8 may be used here with family issues. You may have noted that the structure of dreamwork is very similar in Taub-Bynum's family work to individual dream analysis. I personally prefer to do live dreamwork demonstrations, but have prepared a videotape example which I sometimes use.

What is most important in dreamwork is helping students and professionals realize that the structure of dreamwork is precisely the same as psychodynamic practice. I find there is a tendency among both students and professionals (including experienced psychodynamic practitioners) to see dreamwork separate as a special type of analytic practice.

In my personal conversations with John Bowlby, he told me that the *practice* of attachment theory was essentially that of the psychodynamic approach. In my interpretation, Bowlby would endorse the following five points.

> *1. Client developmental history is important and needs to be considered for full client understanding.* We can learn client developmental history systematically through the Tamase-type life-span review of Chapter 6 or we can simply use the basic listening sequence to draw on past events. As we learn about past events using good client-centered skills, we obtain many important ideas which help explain how present behavior was *learned in the family of origin.* (Thus helping us tie social learning theory to both psychodynamic and family systems work.)

2. *Important in our developmental history are the key people we have related with over time—our object relations.* In addition, multicultural factors influence the course of this developmental history. As part of our developmental listening, we need to *focus* on other key caregivers, particularly the family as it develops in culture. We must never forget MCT's point that we develop in relationship in a cultural setting.

3. *We are unaware (unconscious) of the impact of both biological needs, the impact of past developmental object relations on our present behavior, and of cultural determinants.* Psychodynamic work as described in the following chapter, both individualistic and Taub-Bynum's more culturally aware approach will help develop this awareness. Free association and seeing patterns between our past and present lives is basic to this awareness.

4. *We constantly act out in daily lives our developmental history and our unconscious biological drives.* As we learn to understand developmental history and how it might affect the present, we begin to realize that we are repeating old scripts. This happens most clearly when we examine the genogram of an individual who grew up in an alcoholic family. But many, most likely most, of our clients grew up in dysfunctional families, faced sexism, homophobia, and racism. It is amazing how therapeutic it is to find out how our present behavior has been ruled from past hurt.

As you examine cultural identity theory the psychology of liberation as presented by Freire, you will find that there are real parallels in the discovery process of these theories and the approach to psychodynamic thought presented here. This chapter is an attempt to work with *self-in-relation* to context.

5. *The task of counseling and therapy is to help the client discover the unconscious roots of present behavior.* Through psychodynamic techniques and concepts such as free association, interpretation, and analysis of transference, we can help the client discover and understand the background of present behavior, thoughts, and feelings. These specific techniques are emphasized in the next chapter.

4. Using Psychodynamic Theory for Case Conceptualization. I like to lecture on the main points of these pages even though students may have read them. I then like to divide students into groups while they examine another personality disorder or DSM-III-R problem from this frame of reference. DCT videotapes are available on this model. At least one hour is required for this procedure, but it helps students master the framework more precisely.

Multiple Choice Questions

1. The unconscious as defined by the text is most closely represented by the following statement.

a) those aspects of biological drive of which we are unaware.
b) those aspects of daily experience which are often forgotten.
c) our multicultural experience through our lives.
d) b and c above.
e) all of the above.*

2. Comas-Diaz and Minrath speaking of the multicultural implications of psychodynamic theory

a) encourage us to use these notions as part of therapy.*
b) warn us that sexism is endemic to psychoanalysis and thus this type of therapy should be avoided.
c) points out that MCT is directly antagonistic to this frame of reference.
d) b and c above.
e) none of the above

3. Taub-Bynum stresses that a family orientation to psychodynamic theory can

a) correct traditional errors.
b) help us see how the individual developed in a family and culture context.*
c) replace the individualistic approach of psychoanalysis.
d) allow us to work psychodynamically without the notion of unconscious.

4. Sue and Sue point out that all but one of the following as true.

a) Insight is not valued by many culturally different clients.
b) Many Asian elders believe that thinking too much about something can cause problems.
c) Insight into problems is useless.*
d) Lower socioeconomic groups often don't find insight helpful to their problems.

5. The instinctual pole of personality, particularly important in traditional drive theory.

a) id*
b) ego
c) superego
d) none of the above
e) all of the above

6. Especially important to Erik Erikson's life-span idea—for example, his thoughts about adolescent identity development.

a) id
b) ego*
c) superego
d) none of the above
e) all of the above

7. Attachment theory as presented by Bowlby is oriented to

a) id
b) ego
c) superego
d) none of the above
e) all of the above*

8. The primary place where family and cultural experience reside.

a) id
b) ego
c) superego*
d) none of the above
e) all of the above

9. Bowlby observed children separated from their parents during the London blitz. He found

a) young children soon adapted to the loss of their parents and there seemed to be no lasting impact of the separation.
b) some children greeted their parents enthusiastically and bound to them easily once again, thus indicating a solid early attachment.
c) most children did not greet their parents enthusiastically, rather they edged toward them carefully.*
d) all of them were angry at their parents and the long separation.

10. The text argues defense mechanisms

a) are a way to cover-up past history.
b) are learned throughout our developmental history as ways for us to cope with the world.*
c) are best explained through unconscious theory, particularly id functions.
d) are a result of weak ego functioning.

11. The text claims that antisocial functioning is

a) often a logical response to difficult developmental history.*
b) a result of biological factors.

c) to be expected as a result of poor parenting.
d) a defense mechanism which results from defects in ego functioning.

12. Your client says he can't remember what happened to him in Vietnam. The is most likely the defense mechanism of

a) denial*
b) repression
c) displacement
d) reaction-formation

13. Your veteran client treats his family badly, particularly after having a bad dream the night before.

a) continuation
b) projection
c) displacement*
d) reaction-formation

14. Your client believes that you are angry with him and there is no evidence in your behavior for this and this is also supported by your supervisor. The client's defense mechanism is most likely

a) continuation
b) projection*
c) displacement
d) reaction-formation

15. Your client decides to do volunteer work to help other veterans.

a) identification
b) projection
c) sublimation*
d) reaction-formation

16. Your client develops terrible headaches after his dreams.

a) continuation
b) projection
c) conversion*
d) reaction-formation

17. We associate the following period with issues of trust.

a) oral*
b) anal
c) oedipal
d) latency

18. We associate the following period with issues of control.

a) oral
b) anal*
c) oedipal
d) latency

19. According to the text, the caregiver

a) has been narrowly defined in traditional psychology as the mother and/or the nuclear family.
b) in some cultures is actually the extended family or community.
c) may include the day care worker.
d) a and b above
e) all of the above*

20. In the Strange Situation Procedure these children tend to smile and hug the returning parent.

a) securely attached*
b) anxious resistant
c) anxious/avoidant
d) all of the above

21. In the Strange Situation Procedure these children tend to ignore or even back way from the mother

a) securely attached
b) anxious resistant
c) anxious/avoidant*
d) all of the above

22. The text argues that

a) attachment research only holds true in Eurocentric cultures.
b) the patterns of childhood attachment tend to continue into later life.*
c) autonomy and individuation are the most important issues in development.
d) b and c above.
e) all of the above.

23. All but one of the following are true about Taub-Bynum's work on the family unconscious.

a) It closely parallels traditional Freudian constructs, but adds a new multicultural dimension.*
b) It is more related to the Jungian concepts of the collective unconscious, but from a more family-based framework.

c) It permits culture to become part of psychodynamic theory.
d) We can best understand individuals in a family context.

24. The child is immediately placed on the mother's body at birth and the two molded together as one.

a) a new mode of birthing in California.
b) characteristic of Japanese culture.*
c) a developing trend in hospitals to foster effective attachment.
d) b and c above.
e) all of the above.

25. "The unconscious is the discourse of the Other." The cryptic phrase associated with Lacan means most closely

a) our very life style may be simply what others desire for us.*
b) unconscious mental functioning is very powerful.
c) the language we speak is determined by culture.
d) ego functioning can be made more powerful by awareness of super-ego constructs.

26. Family symptoms we observe, according to Taub-Bynum, may

a) be the repository of the collective unconscious.
b) the result of several generations of family members who themselves may not have shown the symptoms.*
c) need to be considered in relationship to ego functioning, but some attention needs to be given to the superego world as well.
d) a and c above
e) none of the above

27. The text and Taub-Bynum both argue for one of the following when working with psychodynamic theory.

a) stay true to psychodynamic approaches and don't mix in other theories.
b) combine other theories and techniques with your work, particularly those oriented to action rather than just thought.*
c) combine other theories which will help the client gain new points of view on old problems thus gaining increased intentionality.
d) occasionally mix in other theories, but only very occasionally and with considerable forethought.

28. Okun, working from a feminist perspective argues

a) psychodynamic theories are irrelevant with women.
b) we need to look at issues of development from a perspective of gender roles.*

c) psychodynamic theory is less effective than feminist therapy.
d) b and c above.
e) all of the above.

29. The narcissistic client often has a developmental history which includes:

a) being totally ignored as a child.
b) a good deal of interpersonal strife with both parents and siblings.
c) reward of achievements and actions that the parents wanted for him or her.*
d) secure attachment that was overdone resulting in a "spoiled" narcissistic type of style.

30. Dependent clients may have had which of the following in the developmental history?

a) extensive abuse.
b) secure attachment which fostered dependency.
c) dependent behavior modeled by one or more caregivers.*
d) a move to separation when the child was too young.

31. Stiver reinterprets dependency from a feminist framework as

a) a common disorder among women.
b) a process of counting on other people to help with meeting needs.*
c) a result of patriarchal male structures.
d) another example of DSM-III-R's discounting of women.

32. Dependent female clients who take up with narcissistic or antisocial personality styles (male or female) may be predicted, according to the text,

a) to have a good match in that they are with controlling types who will meet their dependency needs.
b) be at risk for suffering physical and emotional abuse.*
c) move very quickly out of the relationship when they realize it isn't good for them.
d) to get "burned" once, but after that, they learn to avoid people of this type.

33. Which type of relationships does the text recommend for the dependent client?

a) firm clear boundaries throughout the process to help the individuation process.

b) looser boundaries at the beginning with a gradual tightening of boundaries and separation later.*
c) start with an enmeshed relationship, then move to rigid boundaries as soon as possible.
d) balance tight and loose boundaries throughout the therapeutic process so that dependent clients will learn how to deal with reality.

Essay Questions

1. Multicultural and feminist writers have presented severe critiques of the psychodynamic frame of reference. Outline the main points of their critiques and write your own position on these critical issues.

2. The chapter on psychodynamic approaches seeks to make this framework more multiculturally relevant through the ideas of John Bowlby, Mary Ainsworth, and Bruce Taub-Bynum. What concepts presented by these authors stand out for you and how would they make psychodynamic theory more culturally relevant?

3. How can the antisocial personality be seen as a "developmental disorder" which is a logical response to developmental history. Given this frame, what does this suggest to you as treatment alternatives?

4. The text presents an unorthodox framework explaining how defense mechanisms arise. What are the main points of this framework and do you agree or disagree?

5. We develop in relationship. Discuss and critique this statement.

6. Outline the essential points of Taub-Bynum's view of the family unconscious.

7. Using the model outlined in the text, discuss the antisocial personality. a) What is the likely developmental history in the family of origin? b) What type of interpersonal relationships would you predict for this individual? c) How is the client likely to function in the work environment? d) As a father or mother, how is this person predicted to treat their own children? e) What treatment recommendations would you make?

SUGGESTED SUPPLEMENTARY READING

Bowlby, J. *A Secure Base: Parent-Child Attachment and Healthy Human Development.* New York: Basic Books, 1988.

This is perhaps the best and most accessible summary of John Bowlby's theorizing and the research which is based on his model. It is an excellent blend of theory with highly practical implications.

Clément, C. *The Lives and Legends of Jacques Lacan.* New York: Columbia, 1983.

The work of Jacques Lacan is obtuse, complex, and subject to varied interpretations. Yet, his reading of the profession of psychoanalysis is very different and challenging from the mainstream. It has profound implications for multiculturally-aware counseling and therapy. This book is a highly literate and sometimes amusing review of Lacan's work. It is a good place to start the Lacanian journey.

Freud, S. *A General Introduction to Psychoanalysis.* Garden City, NY: Doubleday, 1943. (Also available in numerous paperback editions.)

Freud provides the best introduction to his own work and this series of lectures is written in clear prose. Too many read Freud in secondary sources, failing to realize that he is the best presenter of his own ideas.

Greenberg, J., and S. Mitchell. *Object Relations in Psychoanalytic Theory.* Cambridge, MA.: Harvard, 1983.

This is the current most cited text on object relations theory. However, it is considered by many an American ego-psychology interpretation which misses multicultural issues. The book deals with John Bowlby with only a brief discussion and does not consider Alice Miller. Its understanding of Melanie Klein is a failure. Issues of child abuse and cultural factors are not covered in the index. Nonetheless, it is a representative summary of an "establishment" construction of object relations theory. As a professional, it is important that you be able to discuss the world of psychodynamic thought from multiple perspectives.

Ivey, A. (1991) *Developmental Strategies for Helpers: Individual, Family and Network Interventions.* North Amherst, Ma.: Microtraining.

Elaboration of the personality/style disorder material may be found here as well specific suggestions for working with depression and other difficult diagnostic areas.

Masterson, J. The Narcissistic and Borderline Disorders: An Integrated Developmental Approach. New York: Brunner/Mazel, 1981.

Masterson provides one of the best summaries of object relations theory currently available. His discussion of childhood patterns of narcissistic and borderline clients has been highly influential and provides a useful follow-up on the ideas of this chapter. Masterson, like many theorists of the borderline client, gives insufficient attention to issues of childhood sexual abuse and cultural issues.

Miller, A. *The Drama of the Gifted Child.* Basic Books, 1981.

Alice Miller's work is some of the most controversial in the psychodynamic field. She represents that major attack on Freud's phantasy theories and her work is antithetical to much of U.S. ego psychology theory. Her writing style is less scholarly and thus is clearer than other writer in this area (except for Bowlby). As such, this may be one of the reasons that her powerful work tends to be ignored by many professionals. Also, her success in the popular market may also be a hindrance to professional populations.

Chapter 8

Psychodynamic Counseling and Therapy
Part II: Applications for Practice

Overview

This chapter focuses on action and treatment, although several new concepts are presented. The case example, "The Fire Tower" that was used in the second edition of *Counseling and Psychotherapy* has been edited and updated and may be found at the conclusion of this chapter. Again, feel free to duplicate that case if you wish for your students.

The major concepts of this chapter include:

> *1. The importance of free association as a basic technique for psychodynamic counseling and therapy.*
>
> *2. Basic interviewing and treatment techniques including:* interpretation, free association, dream analysis, family dreamwork, regression techniques, analysis of resistance, analysis of transference and counter-transference, and projective identification.
>
> *3. Special attention is given throughout the chapter on treatment of the family/multicultural unconscious.*
>
> *4. A number of culturally-appropriate interventions from a psychodynamic perspective are presented.*

Class Procedures

The general orientation to this chapter is practical and consists primarily of class exercises to illustrate the concepts in action.

1. Free Association: The Past Repeats in the Present. I like to begin the practice of psychodynamic work with some variation of the free association exercise at the beginning of the chapter. In particular, I like to add the gender, family of origin, and cultural/ethnic identification issue to the process. Usually, I simply take the whole class through the exercise and then ask them to write down their impressions in a journal and then share them as they wish with their classmates. We also discuss the theoretical foundations of free association as the basic technique of psychodynamic formulations.

2. Using Psychodynamic Theory for Case Conceptualization. I like to review the personality style/disorder material. It is important to think about psychodynamic theory in terms of case analysis as well as practice.

3. Relationship—Treat Client's Differently Than They Have Been Treated in the Past. In some ways this is a small point, but it is a useful one to help students think about the issue of relationship in psychodynamic therapy and counseling. This also helps students maintain awareness that relationship is important, perhaps even more important in this orientation to helping. What is an effective relationship for one client may not be effective for the next. Depending on client needs, our interviewing relationships must vary. A consistent relational style for all clients may be individually and culturally inappropriate.

4. Interpretation. As the interpretation/reframe skill was covered in the chapter on microskills, it permits time for the multicultural and family interpretations in role-played sessions. Too often psychodynamic counselors make individualistic interpretations and thus miss the underlying family and multicultural dimensions.

5. Expanding Free Association to Multicultural Issues. I have found psychodynamic thought quite compatible with multicultural issues if we keep a balanced *focus* on individual, family, and multicultural issues. The exercise in free association and guided imagery with gender, religious, and cultural symbols is a good class exercise. Again, using microskill-type practice groups, students divide into three's or four's, practice the skill, and then receive feedback from their groups.

In addition, the wide array of free association exercises may be used in the "Free Association Exercises and Techniques" presentation.

6. Dream Analysis. I find the best way to help students understand dream analysis is a live demonstration. But, I have also developed videotape demonstrations through Microtraining. Students are surprised at how well the systematic approach works and how important the discoveries that come out are to the volunteer client.

Particularly important in the success of this exercise is mastery of the imagery concepts of developmental counseling and therapy. Once the students have mastered imagery, they can do free association to earlier life experiences with a sensorimotor foundation. My experience with psychodynamic therapists is that they too often do free association from the concrete or, worse yet, the formal operational level. Small wonder psychodynamic practitioners produce change so slowly! This is sad because the underlying ideas of the model are very useful and very compatible with cognitive-behavioral, Gestalt, and even client-centered approaches. Used with an egalitarian approach, the ideas here are highly useful with MCT and feminist therapy.

Please note that dreamwork techniques suggested here work well with any topic. The brief transcript presented on ACOA's is typical of work that can be done in this area. You will note that this work is also characteristic of "inner child" work and can be an avenue to tie psychodynamic thinking to work with substance abusers.

I always require my students to do a dream analysis or structure an interview using the same model. It seems to be one of the more popular and effective techniques that comes out of the course.

7. The Family Dream and Multicultural Issues. The same procedures as above can be used, but the focus turns to the family and may include multicultural issues as well.

8. Using Regression Techniques to Reexperience Past Trauma. In my advanced courses, I spend at least two sessions this concept. With less experienced trainees, I tend to skip over this material. Regression techniques such as these are some of the most powerful available to us. The model of bringing about regression, of course, closely follows the free association exercise at the beginning of the chapter, but the material is obviously much more loaded emotionally.

Producing regression is not that difficult if you follow DCT and free association guidelines presented here. What is difficult, however, is balancing regression with a sense of ethics and the ability of the client to encounter the trauma once again. That is why we emphasized concrete story telling in the chapter.

9. Analysis of Resistance. Again, I like to do live demonstrations using the techniques of free association and imagery. I see resistance as an opportunity and never as a problem. The exercises on free association in the text provide some additional ideas for practice in analyzing resistance.

10. Analysis of Transference and Counter-Transference. If students have mastered the foundational skills of the first section of this book (particularly basic empathic and microskills, MCT understandings, and DCT skills), they should be able to engage fairly effectively in most of the concepts of this chapter.

Again, I do live demonstrations of these issues, have students observe my behavior for counter Transferential problems, and then debrief with the class what occurred. Students say that the live demonstrations are the most vital part of their growth and understanding.

11. Projective Identification. I find this one of the most difficult and complex concepts. What helps for me is to look at family of origin work and intergenerational transmission of behavioral and emotional characteristics. Behavior learned in the family of origin continues into adult life and we tend to produce certain behaviors and emotions in others. In effect, awareness of transference and counter-transference is not enough. We need to become aware as therapists how clients can enact our own desires without our conscious awareness.

I've been able to produce fairly clear examples of projective identification in some of my live demonstrations, both in terms of my own behavior and the behavior of clients.

12. Treating the Family/Multicultural Unconscious. It seems important to recall that all of the above psychodynamic constructs can be treated from a multicultural frame of reference by *focusing* the intervention on the family or on multicultural issues. Again, the microskill of focus will be helpful in making these constructs multiculturally relevant.

Multiple Choice Questions

1. Alice Miller suggests that counselors are often "nice" because

a) they learn skills of listening in their courses.
b) they are naturally kind people.
c) they have learned the hard way that anger and other methods are ineffective over the long term.
d) their family roles often required them to be "nice" to survive.*

2. The text argues that

a) the most lasting interpretations are ultimately made by the client.*
b) interpretation is the most important skill that a psychodynamic therapist has available.
c) multicultural interpretations are the best, particularly for clients who are culturally different from you.
d) counselors should only use interpretation as a last resort after all other avenues have failed.

3. Which technique does the text consider most foundational to psychodynamic orientations?

a) free association*
b) interpretation
c) analysis of resistance
d) analysis of transference and counter transference
e) projective identification

4. In generating a multicultural image

a) select one that makes sense to the client.
b) coconstruct the image with the client.
c) encourage the client to generate her or his own culturally relevant image.*
d) focus on images which relate to the family of origin.

5. The text argues that dream analysis

a) is similar to techniques of cognitive therapy.
b) is structurally similar to decisional counseling, but the decision here focused on interpretation of the dream.
c) is a set of technique which should be used only with dream.
d) is structurally similar to the general practice of psychodynamic counseling and therapy.*

An African-American client dreams about Martin Luther King's "I had a dream" speech. Classify the following interpretation of the dream.

6. The client has a desire for power.

a) individualistic interpretation*
b) religiously-related interpretation
c) gender-related interpretation
d) Afrocentric interpretation

7. The client is identifying appropriately with a cultural hero.

a) individualistic interpretation
b) religiously-related interpretation
c) gender-related interpretation
d) Afrocentric interpretation*

8. Men always want power.

a) individualistic interpretation
b) religiously-related interpretation
c) gender-related interpretation*
d) Afrocentric interpretation

9. According to the text, which of the above interpretations is most valid?

a) individualistic interpretation
b) religiously-related interpretation
c) gender-related interpretation
d) Afrocentric interpretation
e) all of the above*

10. If you are working with images with a client and they seem overwhelmed by emotion and you aren't quite sure what to do next, the text recommends that you first

a) continue at the sensorimotor level.
b) move to concrete story telling.*
c) look for formal operational patterns in the story.
d) use multicultural focus to help reach the dialectic/systemic level and distance totally from emotion.

11. According to the text and some specialists, Freud contributed to the present abuse of children by

a) ignoring the nature of the child.
b) his phantasy theory of childhood abuse.
c) abandoning his early discoveries on the prevalence of abuse in Vienna.
d) a and b above
e) b and c above.*

12. Freud conceptualized resistance as

a) something to be overcome.
b) the client being unwilling to talk freely.
c) a necessary protective function for the client.*
d) a continually healthy response.

13. "You seem to be responding to me as you did to your mother." This interpretation is likely part of

a) analysis of transference.*
b) analysis of resistance.
c) projective identification.
d) analysis of counter-transference.

14. "It makes sense that you don't want to talk. Could you tell me what comes to mind right now as you look at it." This therapist list is most likely part of

a) analysis of transference.
b) analysis of resistance.*
c) projective identification.
d) analysis of counter-transference.

15. This client seems to bring out immense anger in me and I really don't like to see him.

a) analysis of transference.
b) analysis of resistance.

c) projective identification.*
d) analysis of counter-transference.* (two answers possible here)

16. Concrete story telling in working with trauma survivors, according to the text is

a) critical to wearing away the trauma.*
b) dangerous and to be avoided.
c) not as effective as more distant and safe formal operational analysis and discussion.
d) irrelevant to the social constructivist process of dynamic therapy.

17. Regression techniques, according to the authors

a) are a treatment of choice for all trauma survivors.
b) never should be used due to dangers.
c) are increasingly less controversial due to recent research.
d) should always be used with care, appropriate supervision, and client awareness of issues involved.*

18. The Vanderbilt Psychotherapy Studies found that

a) professionals are the most effective in establish relationships with their clients.
b) professionals are about the same as untrained college professors in establishing relationships with their clients.*
c) college professors are more effective if they are trained carefully.
d) college professors are naturally more effective.

19. The Vanderbilt Psychotherapy Studies found that specific "manualized" procedures

a) made therapy more specific and researchable.
b) made therapists more effective.
c) helped college professors become even more effective.
d) seemed to "get in the way" at times of effective helping relationships.*

20. Senoi dreamwork

a) emphasizes culturally appropriate spiritual symbols.
b) provides evidence that psychodynamic therapy will work in other cultures.
c) is useful only in a culturally specific situation.
d) focuses on finding positive meanings in even the most disturbing dream.*

Essay Questions

1. Regression techniques are increasingly controversial in the field of counseling and therapy. Would you use these techniques? Why or why not? Regardless, what precautions would you recommend to practitioners?

2. Write individual, family, and multicultural interpretations of the following client comment.

> (Irish-American client) I've been having trouble with my wife. She never listens to me. I came home the other night and she had just come home from work. Nothing was on the table. A man has to have his food after he works all day.
>
> (African-American client) I didn't get the job. I thought I had a good interview, but they hired someone else.

3. Outline some of the dangers of free association and imagery techniques when used with regression. How can these be alleviated?

4. Outline the basic structure of a dream analysis and point out how this structure could be used for interpersonal conflict or difficulty at work.

5. Define and provide examples of transference, counter transference, resistance, and projective identification.

6. Define and provide examples of transference, counter transference, resistance, and projective identification as they might be viewed in the transcript "The Fire Tower."

CASE EXAMPLE: THE FIRE TOWER

Psychodynamic counseling can take a variety of forms ranging from daily sessions over five or more years in classical psychoanalysis to short-term, highly directive forms of therapy. Common to all these varying approaches is an interest in seeing how the past affects present behavior, thoughts, and feelings. The psychodynamic counselor can benefit from a study of family therapy as the family of origin is where the client has learned his or her particular behavioral style.

Bob is in the early stages of psychodynamic counseling and has just come in for his third interview. Bob's presenting problem was his lack of interest in his family, vague feelings of anxiety, and a general lack of involvement in his job. He is 32, a college graduate, and works as an architect. He is married and has one child, age 2. The psychodynamic counselor is non-traditional and oriented to short-term (twenty to thirty sessions) treatment. (It might be pointed out that short-term treatment in other schools of counseling often range from one to five interviews.)

As is typical of many people who enter this approach to therapy, Bob is highly verbal and intellectual and begins to talk just as soon as he sits down. This is an edited portion of a real interview.

1. Bob: Things seem to be going better. I was able to get the blueprints worked out on the apartment complex. Sue hasn't been on me as much lately. Things are pretty good.

2. Counselor: So, things are pretty good . . . (Minimal encourage)

3. Bob: (Fumbling) . . . I really did a good job on the apartment. Even the boss said so. I really should show you what I did to see what you think. . . (pause) Yeh, things are going pretty well. This weekend I even took Sue and Sonny for a hike.

Bob is searching for an appropriate topic for the interview. Some possible topics for therapist-client discussion include Bob's relationship with his boss, the weekend hike, and his comment that he "should show" the therapist what he did. Here, in the very first part of the session we see Bob treating the therapist as he himself was treated, a clear example of transference.

4. Counselor: Uh-hummm.

This minimal encourager suggests that Bob continue this line of thinking. It may be anticipated that he will continue talking about the hike. This is an illustration that minimal encouragers have important influence on client talk in the interview. Some believe that the last topic presented by a client in a list of problems or issues is the most important. It likely too early in the treatment series to focus on Bob's relationship with the therapist.

5. Bob: Yeh, it was a real change. I haven't done anything like that for ages. We had a real good time, but one funny thing happened when we got to the fire tower near Iron Mountain . . . (pauses, looks to the Counselor).

It may be noted that Bob is talking about a past event which is highly characteristic of psychodynamic approaches. Some other theories would be more interested in his present feelings and thoughts in this interview. Others might be concerned with his behaviors in the specific situation. Ultimately, what is most important in psychodynamic counseling is helping the client become aware of how past events, particularly from childhood, relate to what is happening in daily life.

While Bob is talking about a past event, note that he is looking to the therapist for encouragement, another here and now example which indicates that somehow the client is reacting to the therapist as he did to someone in the past.

6. Counselor: Uh-hummm.

This second minimal encourager concludes the first decisional phase of this interview. Client and counselor have already negotiated what they are to talk about for the next several comments. The hike and then the "funny thing" on the fire tower are to be the major topics of this interview. With the next comment, we move to the work phase of the interview.

7. Bob: Well, what happened was really strange. We climbed up the tower after lunch—we had even done some singing—and when we got to the top, I started to enjoy the fantastic view. Then, I noticed I had placed Sonny on the rail and a panic suddenly came over me.

8. Counselor: Bob, can you get an image of the situation. Can you see you and Sonny on the tower.

It would have been possible to focus on the panic feelings and talk *about* them. Through the use of images, past experience can be brought more to the here and now. In this way, the therapist can become more aware of the depth and meaning of client experience.

9. Bob: (Closes his eyes and is silent. The therapist notes that Bob's body tenses during the process and his hands become tight fists.)

10. Counselor: Stay with that image and the feeling of panic and tell me more about it. What are you seeing and feeling?

The therapist offers a clear directive in the present tense and asks the client to talk about the past in more concrete detail.

11. Bob: Well, I was . . . (Suddenly with greater strength) The panic and tension are all over me, I'm almost shaking now. I was so afraid that Sonny would fall. (Opens eyes) I wanted him to hold me . . . I mean I wanted to hold him close. Wow . . . I wonder what that means.

The client responded to the directive to use imagery with stronger emotion in the here and now. As emotion gets stronger, unconscious feelings are more likely to appear. In this case we see a "Freudian slip" ("I wanted him to hold me . . .") that is rich in potential meaning. Some psychodynamic counselors might pay close attention to that slip and interpret it immediately, even making a decision to make that slip the new key surface structure sentence for exploration. Others might simply note the slip and move forward.

12. Counselor: Well, let's try. Stay with that image and the feeling of panic and fright and then let your mind run free to your earliest memories possible and tell me the first scene that comes to your mind. But first Bob, get with the image again and allow yourself to feel the panic in your body.

13. Bob: (Silence as he goes through the imagery. Again he tightens up.)

14. Counselor: Where do you feel the tension in your body?

15. Bob: In my neck, right here (points).

16. Counselor: Focus on that feeling in your neck and think back on your early life. What come to your mind?

The Counselor uses another directive and asks the client to free associate back to earlier experiences. Free association, the process of letting the mind run free to whatever recollection occurs, is basic to most psychodynamic approaches. Note the strong emphasis on past-tense experience which is reached through observation of the client's present-tense world. The counselor is searching for how present thoughts, feelings, and action are related to the developmental history of the client.

17. Bob: (Quiet for a moment, his eyes drop to the floor as if in trance. Focused free association can be extremely powerful and needs to be use with care, especially when used for age regression.) I see myself driving up Trail Ridge Road in Rocky Mountain Park. We've come to an overlook and we stop. I was about 5 or 6. Dad was a real "card" at the time. I remember him fooling around on the rail at the drop-off. He got up and started walking on it. I remember Mom and I being in acute panic as we watched him. Then, he lost his balance and almost fell. When he was able to get himself down, he was white as a sheet. I was so scared I almost pee'd in my pants.

It should be noted that Bob is a highly verbal and facile client. This is typical of those who stay with psychodynamic therapy. Those less verbally oriented may find free association and the analytical process difficult and often drop out. Bob is able to be very concrete about his past experience and it is fairly easy to see the parallels between his feelings for his father and for his own son. This parallel is particularly important in object relations theory.

18. Counselor: So, when you were up in the fire tower with Sonny you had a real panicked feeling, and when your father almost fell you had similar feelings.

The therapist offers a summary in which father-son feelings in both situations are mentioned. It would be possible for the counselor to make the interpretation for the client directly. However, most prefer that the client eventually interpret her or his own personal experience. Psychodynamic theory holds that present reactions to people stem from important past situations. In this example, Bob has feelings toward his son similar to those he felt toward his own father.

You will note that Bob's Freudian slip focused on his desire to have his son hold him. Unfortunately, parents often use children to act out their unconscious wishes. If Bob continues this type of unconscious thought in relationship to his son, the possibility of producing a "parentified" placating, peacemaking child is there.

In counseling and therapy sessions, you will find that you are often working with three or more generations of the family system, even though you are working with an individual. The importance of reworking old trauma thus becomes even more important so that intergenerational transmission of distress is prevented.

19. Bob: Yeh . . . ?

The client is unable to make the connections between the two situations. If a direct interpretation of the parallel had been made, it may be anticipated that he would have rejected it. Interpretations are only effective when the client is ready to hear them. Interpretations are often most lasting if the client makes the connections him or herself.

20. Counselor: Right now, I see your hand shaking.

This feedback is in the present tense and gives special attention to nonverbal communication. Some psychodynamic therapists would never directly refer to nonverbal communication at all while others might use it extensively.

21. Bob: I'm feel panicked right now as a I talk with you. What does it all mean?

Very common to psychodynamic clients and therapists is the search for what an event, behavior, or situation "means." The search for meaning is almost always in the past. It is on this specific issue that humanistically oriented third-force psychology would criticize this interview. They would be more concerned with the client's present experience of the world and give scant attention to its derivation from the past. A Gestalt therapist might ask Bob to imagine his father in an empty chair and direct Bob to share his thoughts and feelings with the chair.

22. Counselor: You're confused and puzzled. What do you think it means?

The therapist first reflects here and now immediate feelings and follows this with an open question. The counselor is seeking to have Bob make the connections in his own time.

23. Bob: (Relaxing a little) I did seem to have the same feelings with Sonny as I did when I was with my folks (pause) . . . the same feeling of panic . . . both were high places and I never have liked high places.

Building on the prompting from the therapist, Bob begins to put together an explanation for his feelings with Sonny. As he relaxes, his body and thought processes become more genuine and integrated or "together." For the first time in this interview, he is beginning to describe parallels in his situation. He is becoming more intentional.

24. Counselor: Right, you do seem to have the same feelings in both settings. Could it be that somehow you are reliving some of your thoughts about your own father right now?

This is basically an interpretation on the part of the therapist. He paraphrases Bob's last comment and seems to be asking an open question. However, the open question is really a tentative interpretation. Tentativeness in interpretation allows the client room to accept or reject the therapist's ideas and avoids a confrontation between them if the interpretation is too soon or incorrect. This also shows respect for the client.

Important also in this interpretation is the linking of past and present experience. Observation suggests that the most effective psychodynamic counseling interventions are those which help the client see how he or she may be reliving the past in the present.

25. Bob: My god! My father never would have anything to do with me. He never showed any interest in me. That trip was one of the few times he stopped working to be with me. He died shortly after that trip, you know . . . (hesitates)

This could be termed the moment of insight. Bob begins to see at a deep emotional level how his father still has a very real grip on his daily life even though his father died years ago. A host of psychodynamic alternative hypotheses could be raised at this point. Among many others are the relationship between resentment toward Bob's absent father and the distance Bob has with Sonny, the feelings of love and anger held toward both, the fear of death being associated with close emotional experience (his father almost fell when things were going well, then he died shortly after a pleasant trip; and the vague anxiety surrounding Sonny on the fire tower), etc. This vast array of possible areas to explore partially explains the long duration of this approach to therapy. It is apparent that for major changes to occur with Bob (at least from this point of view), he must work through many, many experiences and connect them with the past.

26: Counselor: (Silence)

27: Bob: Dad died shortly after that (tears start). The funeral was awful, but I didn't cry. I just sat there blankly. Everyone said I was so brave and like a "little man." (Wipes eyes.) I guess that's the way I'm supposed to be—take care of everyone.

There are also gender and cultural issues in this case. We see cultural demands placed on a male child to "be brave" and "little man." The failure to recognize and acknowledge grief and loss, particularly in the sensitive child (or adult) can result in repression. But, psychodynamic theory reminds us that even though the events are repressed, emotionally they remain in the mind and body at an unconscious level. The very work psychodynamic implies activity and when Bob felt panic with his son, we see the dynamic activity from his unconscious thought processes.

28. Counselor: So to sum up to this point, it seems plausible that somehow the experience with Sonny on the tower relates back to your earlier experiences with your own father. A while back you commented that you wanted to hold your son close on the tower. Before that, do you remember what you said—just before that?

The therapist believes that the connections between father and son and father and son are clear to Bob and starts to recycle the interview back for more work. His summary of the interview to this point is accurate, but fails to take into account the present-tense confusion of the client. It would have been preferable to let Bob discuss more feelings about his father. The therapist in this case did not want to move to depth implications of Bob's relationship, so suggested recycling back to the Freudian slip. If the client had been ready, this could have been most effective in uncovering more clearly the parallels between the two relationships.

This is an error which can be all too common in psychodynamic approaches which focus on insight. The client is still very much in an emotional state and needs to work things through more completely. Some therapists, too, are uncomfortable with tears and client emotional expression and "save" their clients. The therapeutic error that Alice Miller stresses in her book, *The Drama of the Gifted Child* (1981), that many of us enter the helping profession to "find ourselves" and in this process often protect ourselves and our clients from earlier childhood pain.

29. Bob: (A blank look comes over his face) No. Why?
The client was not ready for recycling back to an earlier point. The Counselor would have been more effective by staying with Bob at this

emotional moment of discovery. However, errors occur in all interviews and the counselor can still salvage the loss. It is not the errors we make, it is the recovery skills we have to correct errors that are most important.

30. Counselor: I think I took you off-track. Let's go back to the funeral. You were saying you were brave and didn't cry. Do you have an image of the funeral? What comes to mind?

(The interview continues . . .) This is a classic illustration of the use of simple attending behavior skills to work with a difficult situation. Generally it is best to admit errors of focus or timing and then to use attending skills to help return to the world of the client. An axiom of the basic microskill of attending behavior is: *When you or the client become lost and confused, return to something said earlier in the interview and start again.*

Additional Interview Analysis

Microskills of the therapist included minimal encouragers, directives, reflection of feeling/paraphrasing, feedback, self-statement, interpretations, and summarization. An orthodox psychoanalyst would be expected to use primarily interpretation due to the belief that other verbal statements tend to direct the client.

The hope of psychodynamic approaches is to free the client to explore the world in her or his own unique fashion through free association. This is in the expectation that basic life patterns will reveal themselves with minimal therapist direction. In truth, most psychodynamic counselors will use skills other than pure interpretation to help move the client ahead faster; yet these other skills are invariably oriented toward interpretation and the generation of new meanings from the psychodynamic framework.

Often the most powerful and meaningful interpretations are based on the nonverbal behaviors of the client. The therapist at 20 did not interpret Bob's behavior, but the observation clearly affected the direction of the session. If you have a good relationship, commenting on and providing feedback on nonverbal behaviors brings here and now issues to the fore.

Transferential issues appear in the interview at the beginning of the session where Bob seems to be attempting to please the counselor. Very possibly, Bob is reacting to the counselor in some way that is similar to the way he interacts with his wife, his son, and—early on—his own parents. John Bowlby reminds us that children learn basic patterns of attachment and behavior in relationship to their caregivers which repeat again and again throughout the life span.

The focused free association techniques can be used to work with issues of transference in the immediacy of the session. However, you as counselor or therapist need to feel quite secure before focusing in this area. Essentially, you can work on issues of transference with a client such as Bob through noting their nonverbal and verbal reactions to you, commenting on them, and then asking the client to generate on image free associated from the here and now interaction with you. As the client gradually learns that past developmental history is being played out again with you, there is the opportunity for re-experiencing the past in a new, safer and more controlled situation.

It is here that you are particularly important. Instead of treating Bob as he was treated in his family of origin or by his culture at the funeral, you can treat him differently. Specifically, you can encourage relevant expression of emotion about people and situations and toward you. You can give feedback and support for new ways of thinking, feeling, and behaving. Some from the psychodynamic orientation talk about the therapist "reparenting" the client, allowing them to express thoughts and feelings in new, more effective ways.

You will find that the approach to psychodynamic counseling suggested in this chapter can be greatly enriched through timely addition of other therapeutic theories and techniques. For example, Gestalt repetition can help a highly intellectualized client to feel more in the here and now. The solid Rogerian relationship seems essential if you are to win client trust. Cognitive and behavior techniques can be used to help clients analyze and understand present ways of behaving and to practice new modes of being.

The chapters on developmental counseling and therapy and family therapy provide conceptual frames and techniques which may help you see the client in her or his context. Finally, multicultural counseling theory and method remind us that clients develop differently in varying cultures. The basic framework of psychodynamic counseling seems to have cultural relevance, but must be adapted to meet varying client needs and experiences.

SUGGESTED SUPPLEMENTARY READING

Taub-Bynum, E.B. (1984) *The Family Unconscious.* Wheaton, IL.: Quest.

Taub-Bynum, E.B. (1992) *Family Dreams: The Intracate Web.* Ithaca, N.Y.: Haworth Press.

> Taub-Bynum, perhaps more than anyone else, has helped make psychodynamic theory culturally relevant. Students are fascinated by his work which suggests many ways to include family and cultural issues in the practice of counseling and therapy.

Chapter 9

Cognitive-Behavioral Therapy and Counseling, Part I Behavioral Foundations

Overview

It is no longer easy to separate behavioral psychology from cognitive-behavioral orientations. The work of Meichenbaum and others has provided us with an important synthesis. While introducing the cognitive-behavioral orientation, this chapter focuses primarily on traditional behavioral interventions. We move in more detail to the cognitive orientation in the next chapter.

In teaching this material, I find that students really appreciate my nuts and bolts pragmatic approach. I ask them to conduct an applied behavioral analysis, engage in a number of the practical techniques, and generate their own stress management program. With advanced classes, I ask them to teach stress management to some group.

Major concepts covered in this chapter include:

> *1. The evolving cognitive-behavioral worldview.* The move toward a more humanistic CBT is presented. The multiple reality worldview of CBT as presented by Meichenbaum is quite similar to MCT and DCT frames, and even includes increasing sensitivity to multicultural issues.
>
> *2. Multicultural issues* are especially important to consider in this chapter. My reading of the literature is that Donald Cheek very early on presented us with a culturally relevant CBT. Unfortunately, the world was not ready for Cheek's advanced thinking in 1976. We like to think that now it is.
>
> *3. Applied behavioral analysis.* After all these years, we have come to respect these methods of case analysis even more. Functional analysis seems critical for us regardless of theoretical orientation of the clinician or counseling, as they seem to help students understand how to make concrete sense of many diverse therapeutic and counseling issues.
>
> *4. Meichenbaum's construction of CBT provides an excellent theoretical integration of the many ideas of the book.* While we have selected MCT as our integrative frame, Meichenbaum's latest writing is nicely metatheoretical and a highly pragmatic way to view the field.

5. The research and clinical summary on agoraphobia should be helpful as a way to integrate the ideas of Meichenbaum.

6. The practice of CBT. Here we present a number of important treatment activities: pinpointing behavior, positive reinforcement, charting, relaxation training, biofeedback, systematic desensitization, modeling, social skills training, assertiveness training, relapse prevention, and stress inoculation and stress management.

Class Procedures

The microskills approach to teaching the concepts of this chapter is helpful. I often do live modeling of the techniques or show a film and then have students practice them in small groups. If practice time is not available, I have students do homework in which they actually engage in the technique. Given the above, my class procedures are a bit different here than in the other chapters and the outline below reveals that fact.

1. The Evolving Cognitive-Behavioral Worldview, The Multicultural Approach, and Meichenbaum's Construction of Cognitive-Behavioral Therapy. I do like to present my impressions of these points to the students via a brief lecture and then discuss with them their impressions of the behavioral movement. As we all do, I like to share the history of the fights between behaviorism and humanistic, the Rogers-Skinner debate, and the like. But, all the time emphasizing that these arguments are for the more part now history. The task for the future is to generate a CBT which is consonant with multicultural needs and facilitative to an integrative counseling and therapy.

2. Applied Behavioral Analysis. The following model is helpful in clarifying these important constructs. Note that I follow the basic microskills models in this training.

Introduction and cognitive structure. I like to ask students what they already know about applied behavioral analysis and list it on the board. I like to stress the importance of relationship variables and listening skills as part of the process of applied behavioral analysis. I give particular attention to the importance of an *egalitarian* approach to this area. Our task is to work *with* not *on* clients. We can do this best by making clients co-investigators with us in the process.

The language of behavioral counseling is by and large very concrete with a minimum of formal operations abstractions. I remind students of the importance of concreteness in terms of facilitative conditions, microskills, and concrete operations in DCT.

Modeling. A student volunteer serves as a real or role-played client and I work through the A-B-C's of a problem or situation with them. It is best to videotape your demonstration and then use that to debrief the interview. If my class is more experienced, I may have a student practice ahead of time and do the modeling instead of me, thus making the concepts perhaps even more relevant.

Didactic. If the students need more specifics, this is the time to present the A-B-C's, the questions, and objectives that go with each part of the framework. If the students are more advanced, this may not be necessary.

Practice. Students practice the framework in small groups with an observer. If possible these small groups may be videotaped.

Generalization. Students are assigned homework in which they do another A-B-C analysis.

3. Agoraphobia: CBT Assessment and Treatment. I like to begin this presentation by asking the students to recall the network treatment plan of Attneave from MCT and the cognitive/emotional developmental levels of DCT. I then play an audiotape by Aaron Beck (good tape available from Guilford) or present a case study which illustrates many of the points of the research box on agoraphobia. The treatment model can be viewed as a variation of network therapy in that a set of treatments which cover multiple cognitive-emotional levels is assembled. For example, the following techniques can be integrated for a systematic treatment program for agoraphobia.

Sensorimotor: Relaxation training, using images to recreate a panic situation or a situation from the past and for a desensitization hierarchy, *in vivo* exposure to situations, careful consideration of medication.

Concrete: A-B-C analysis to bring out concrete specifics of current problem and, often, the developmental history of the problem. Assertiveness to help usually inhibited clients interact more effectively, social skills training, desensitization hierarchy (which is simultaneously sensorimotor), and stress training.

Formal: Self-esteem and self-efficacy training, examining patterns of thought, feeling, and behavior which reoccur (especially the connections between childhood developmental learnings and present issues). Cognitive work as presented in the following chapter (Ellis, Beck), dream analysis as in the psychodynamic chapter, and client-centered therapy.

Dialectic/systemic: Family therapy, marital counseling, examination of family origin via genogram, feminist counseling, consciousness-raising as in MCT's cultural identity theory as appropriate. Special attention is paid here to the context in which agoraphobia may have developed.

If you review the above conception, you may note that depression, borderline personality, and many other issues troubling clients can be conceptualized within the above paradigm. Furthermore, *individual* work is often not enough. Thus, there is need to consider Attneave's broadly-based network constructs as a way to help ensure that new behavior, thought, and feelings are learned and generalized.

5. Techniques and Strategies of CBT. As time permits, I like to work through the specific methods of CBT. I may do live modeling, play an audiotape of a relaxation session, I may present a case and have them develop a concrete treatment plan using these techniques. Students often practice the techniques in microskills-type groups. But I always require them to **do** the techniques even beyond practice in the classroom. I find that students simply read and forget, but if I require them to find a volunteer (usually from the class) that they come back and say, "Well, I didn't think (insert techniques here) would work, but it did and the volunteer client really liked it and seems to be engaged in some change."

Typically, I require the following as a minimum:

1. A written report on applied behavioral analysis.
2. Development of a relaxation training tape and testing it on a client.
3. A written report on establishing a systematic desensitization hierarchy with a client.
4. Teaching some social skill or communication skill, often conducting a microskills workshop with written report and evaluation by participants.
5. A written report on an assertiveness case.
6. The development in writing of a stress management program. With advanced students, they are asked to teach it.
7. Present a multicultural and gender critique on all these activities.

6. Stress Inoculation and Stress Management. If time permits, I like to take my students through a short stress management program which I have developed. This usually includes topics such as the following: 1) discussion and analysis of a specific stressor in their lives in small groups; 2) relaxation training; 3) brief assertiveness training; 4) decision skills from Chapter 3, often a balance sheet; 5) cognitive analysis using the concepts of Chapter 10 (for example a Beck automatic thoughts review or the Ellis A-B-C-D-E-F) or I may use cognitive ideas from a standard book on stress management, widely available everywhere; and

6) relapse prevention. At times, I may add charting as a way to make relapse even more precise.

I then ask students to write their own stress management program and test it out.

7. Psychodynamic Theory and CBT. The field talks about relating CBT to psychodynamic formulations, but it seldom happens. In my courses, I often like to show some connections and the following seems to be helpful:

a) Psychodynamic case conceptions are often helpful in planning an A-B-C analysis. If you examine the developmental history of a depressed or dependent client, for example, you will often find a clear learning history which relates to the current problem. As I note in the book, many clients have histories of trauma which help us understand how the clinical syndrome developed. Psychodynamic theory helps us reach these issues more rapidly and gives us a developmental framework to understand what happened and how it relates to the present.

b) Clearly the highly verbal approach to understanding a client does not always produce change. For those students who seem especially fond of psychodynamic theory, it is very helpful to them to realize that a relaxation training exercise or a desensitization hierarchy may be more helpful to a troubled client at this moment that further verbal analysis. *There is no reason that a student cannot conceptualize psychodynamically, yet engage in effective CBT.* The time or arguing which theory is best is over—the issue now is helping out clients as much as possible.

8. MCT, CBT, and Psychodynamic Theory. Even putting these three in the same title almost seems difficult. But, unless we consider cultural and contextual issues as we conduct either of the traditional theories, we may do damage to African-American, Italian-American, Gay, aged, etc. clients. Psychotherapy would be helped if we started and perhaps ended as well with awareness of multicultural issues.

9. Relapse Prevention. We find it helpful to begin this section with a lecture on the importance of generalization and maintenance of behavior. RP can be useful with all interviews, not just cognitive-behavioral. We would then role-play an interview in front of the class demonstrating the RP concepts followed by them doing the same for further practice and mastery. Finally, we would follow-up the next week to see if relapse has been prevented.

Moreover, you may want to use the RP form as the final stage of the practice five-stage interview. In this way you can integrate RP and the five-stages. The more practice people have with this skill, the more likely it is to be maintained and actually used.

Multiple Choice Questions

1. The case example of the professor who received attention from students, thus shaping his behavior is an example of

a) charting
b) systematic sensitization
c) pinpointing behavior
d) positive reinforcement*

2. Self-efficacy as defined by Bandura is closely related to which concept?

a) desensitization
b) intentionality*
c) cultural limitations
d) multiple perspectives

3. Feminist critiques of CBT include

a) the emphasis on the individual fails to note contextual issues.*
b) its failure to be intentional.
c) that the emphasis on control is antithetical to the women's movement.
d) more action to help individual women is necessary.

4. An early author who pioneered in CBT, according to the text, and was not recognized originally was:

a) Albert Bandura
b) Donald Cheek*
c) Donald Meichenbaum
d) Aaron Beck

5. Shows us how to make CBT multiculturally more relevant:

a) Albert Bandura
b) Donald Cheek*
c) Donald Meichenbaum
d) Aaron Beck

6. The Sloane, et al. study compared psychodynamic and behavioral therapists and found:

a) behavioral therapists were significantly more cold and distant in the interview.

b) psychodynamic therapists were significantly more cold and distant.
c) Rogerian counselors were consistently the warmest helpers.
d) behavioral therapists were as warm or warmer than psychodynamic therapists.*

7. When we operationalize behavior, it helps if we focus more on which dimensions?

a) sensorimotor
b) concrete*
c) formal operational
d) dialectic/systemic

8. In conducting a functional analysis, you may ask, "What happened specifically? What words did he/she use? What happened next?" These example questions are at what level typical of functional analysis?

a) sensorimotor
b) concrete*
c) formal operational
d) dialectic/systemic

Which of the following counselor statements are oriented to antecedents (A), behavior which occurred (B), or which are consequences (C)?

C 9. How did you feel when the argument was over?

A 10. Describe the scene of the argument. Where was it?

B 11. What did you do?

B 12. What did he do?

B 13. What happened next?

A 14. Who came up to you?

C 15. Where did you find yourself afterwards?

16. The text argues that in establishing behavioral change goals for CBT we need to:

a) find the best goals for the client.
b) define them clearly for the client.
c) involve the client as a full participant with us.*
d) only allow the client to participate if he or she is able.

17. Which statement about emotions can be attributed to Meichenbaum?

a) Emotions cause cognitions.
b) Cognitions cause emotions.
c) Cognitions and emotions are part of an interactive process.*
d) all of the above.

18. Meichenbaum feels this about relationship variables in counseling and therapy.

a) It is critical to the change process.*
b) Behavioral counseling can be effective regardless of the relationship which occurs between client and therapist.
c) Relationship is of moderate importance, but an effective behavioral therapist can "make it" even in difficult relationships.
d) Behavioral counselors can be as warm as client-centered.

19. Meichenbaum is relatively unique among behavioral approaches to helping by emphasizing:

a) family therapy and counseling.
b) multicultural issues.
c) relationship issues.
d) all of the above.*
e) none of the above.

20. Agoraphobia

a) is more prevalent in men than in women.
b) is more prevalent in women than in men.*
c) is equally represented by gender.
d) tends to occur more often in children than in adulthood.

21. Agoraphobia is now being related to

a) multicultural discrimination and prejudice.
b) social class.
c) borderline personality disorder.
d) school phobia.*

22. A useful treatment for agoraphobia, according to research findings.

a) psychodynamic dream analysis.
b) client-centered therapy.
c) rational disputation
d) graduated exposure to anxiety provoking situations.*

23. Relaxation training is a sensorimotor technique which appears to be helpful as part of treatment for

a) agoraphobia.

b) depression.
c) anxiety disorders.
d) a and b above.
e) all of the above.*

24. Systematic desensitization consists of which three primary steps?

a) relaxation training, anxiety hierarchies, and charting
b) anxiety hierarchies, stress management, and charting
c) reinforcement, relaxation, and stress management
d) relaxation training, anxiety hierarchies, and matching objects of anxiety with relaxation.*

25. The microskills framework of Chapter 3 can also be considered

a) part of a stress management program.
b) as a focus for social skills training for patients.
c) as a system for functional analysis.
d) a and b above.*
c) all of the above.

26. Ivey found that microskill training with institutionalized psychiatric patients

a) was a useful adjunct to traditional treatment.
b) by itself was effective enough to help patients move out of the hospital who had been institutionalized up to four years.*
c) is a useful part of social skills training.
d) helps them become more assertive.

27. Cheek argues the multicultural factors need to be part of assertiveness training. All but one of the following are part of his contributions to the area.

a) with some cultures, assertiveness training simply doesn't work.
b) African-Americans style of assertion varies from European-Americans.*
c) assertiveness training can be more effective if it involves cognitive work as well.
d) didactic instruction for clients can be helpful as part of assertiveness training.

28. In working with rape survivors, Foa and others found

a) stress management was the most effective treatment.
b) supportive counseling was most effective.
c) repeated imagery and discussing the rape scene itself was most effective.*

d) all of the above together make the most effective treatment program.

29. Research on relapse prevention reveals

a) the client's response to the original lapse is particularly important in the likelihood of future and continued lapses.*
b) it is very difficult to predict which clients will relapse and which won't.
c) that RP is more effective if combined with other theories.
d) support of others is relatively unimportant in lapses.

30. Eye movement desensitization and reprocessing

a) focuses mainly on eye movements.
b) encompasses psychodynamic as well as CBT principles.
c) is a cognitive technique.
d) utilizes many different strategies and, as such, has many aspects in common with developmental counseling and therapy.*

Essay Questions.

1. Design a stress management program which you might use with women who may face sexual harrassment on the job.

2. The cognitive-behavioral frame of reference is often accepted by minority clients in this society as concrete and helpful. What are some multicultural cautions which need to be considered in using this set of techniques?

3. Imagine you are talking with a couple and one of the members has verbally abused the other, at least according to the partner. How would you go about conducting a functional analysis of the verbal abuse?

4. Imagine you are seeing a client with examination anxiety. Construct a desensitization hierarchy as it might appear. How would you use that hierarchy to facilitate treatment?

5. Design a comprehensive behavioral program from the treatment of a client who seem to manifest DSM-III-R characteristics of dependency.

6. How would you adapt the constructs of cognitive-behavioral therapy for children?

7. Behavioral change which is not planned for generalization is likely to be behavioral change which is lost and lamented. How would you develop a relapse prevention program for your clients?

SUGGESTED SUPPLEMENTARY READING

Annual Review of Behavior Therapy: Theory and Practice. New York: Guilford, annual publication.

> Behavior therapy has established itself as a major and permanent member of the helping establishment. This annual volume is important not only as a history of theory and practice, but also as a place to learn new techniques and research and their value in daily work.

Bower, S. A. *Painless Public Speaking.* Glasgow: Thorsons, 1990.

> A cognitive-behavioral approach to speaking in public by the author of the case study on assertiveness discussed in this chapter.

Bower, S. A. and Bower, G. *Asserting Yourself: A Practical Guide for Positive Change.* Reading, MA: Addison-Wesley, 1976. (Now at 18 printings.)

> A guide to assertiveness training, written by the author of the case study presented in this chapter. An especially strong feature of this highly regarded book is its emphasis on demonstrated and lasting change. This classic work has become a standard of the field.

Meichenbaum, D. *Stress Innoculation Training.* New York: Pergammon, 1985.

> The basic guide to stress programs which has had a wide influence internationally. Virtually all counselors and therapists need to have stress management as part of their basic skill repertoire.

Skinner, B. F. *Science and Human Behavior.* New York: Macmillan, 1953.

> The prime architect of behavioral psychology presents an overview of his methods and how they might be applied to a wide array of situations ranging from individual change to systematic change in cultures.

Wolpe, J., and Lazarus, A. *Behavior Therapy Techniques.* Elmsford, NY: Pergamon Press, 1966.

> Although now long out of print, this book remains by far the best and clearest compendium of behavioral techniques. It is a classic which is well worth the search.

Chapter 10

Cognitive-Behavioral Counseling and Therapy: Cognitive and Integrative Approaches

Overview

Again, my teaching in this chapter focuses on students being able to demonstrate some of the main constructs of this chapter. I find that if they have mastered applied behavioral analysis from the preceding chapter that exercises in REBT, cognitive, and reality therapy are readily understood and, for many, mastered at a beginning level.

I also find that students who have mastered foundational skills really can move very rapidly with the material in these chapters.

This chapter presents the work of Ellis, Beck, and Glasser with their central theoretical formulations in the following structure. A major difference in this chapter from the preceding edition is that we have shown more clearly how to adapt CBT theory to include multicultural issues.

> *1. People "are disturbed not by events but by the views they take of them."* Epictetus' statement forms the foundation of this chapter. If students internalize the importance of these words, they seem much more ready to learn and internalize the constructs presented here.
>
> *2. Multicultural issues* are important in this chapter, especially because the cognitive orientation has not been viewed favorably by those writing from a gender or multicultural orientation. There is need to pay special attention to these critiques throughout this chapter and to examine our suggestions as to how CBT might become more inclusive.
>
> *3. Presentations on REBT, cognitive therapy, and reality therapy provide the main bulk of the chapter.* The information on these theorists is presented in the following format:
>
> > Introduction to the theory
> > Case presentation with a transcript
> > Central theoretical constructs and techniques
> > Special considerations
>
> *4. Arnold Lazarus' integrative approach, multimodal therapy ends the two chapter series.* We find that this approach at this point in the text helps students review what they have learned thus far and integrate the many approaches and techniques of CBT.

Class Procedures

1. The Cognitive Worldview. Divide the students into discussion groups and, when they are ready, introduce Epictetus' classic statement to them for discussion. Sometimes, I simply have them talk about their ideas and reactions to Epictetus and these discussions have been fruitful as an introduction to the chapter theorists. I have also asked them to think back on a personal difficulty that they have had or have experienced. Often, after time, we find ourselves reframing that experience in a new context and "changing our view of events." If students can share some of their own very real experiences with changing ideas about things over time, this provides a very helpful way for the class to think about the cognitive approach.

Interpretation, reframing, and the cognitive worldview. I also like to return to the microskill of interpretation/reframing and discuss with the class how these skills are often essential parts of the cognitive reframing process. Ellis, in particular, often uses "why" questions as a way to understand underlying cognitive structures. This is a good place to re-emphasize that varying microskills and empathic conditions are all oriented to helping clients gain a new view of things. In fact, the Third Edition of *Microcounseling* will focus on microskills as a technology of constructivism. The new *Basic Influencing Skills* (1997) provides very concrete ideas for using constructivist concepts in counseling and therapy.

2. Multicultural issues in Cognitive Therapy. Cognitive therapy, by its very nature, focuses on the individual making decisions alone. There is a minimal attention to contextual issues which places cognitive therapy at a considerable distance from multicultural counseling and therapy. Ellis probably the most multiculturally sensitive due to his long history of advocacy for a variety of oppressed groups. But even here, Ellis emphasizes learning to cope with reality rather than changing it.

I tend to lecture briefly on the above point indicating that we need to return to it as we view the work of the three authors. It is also important to note that Meichenbaum's broader construction of CBT in the preceding chapter allows much more room for contextual issues and action in the environment.

Nonetheless, this does not mean that these theories are not important in a multicultural world. We indeed do need to understand that varying cultures have differing view of the same event. In this sense, cognitive therapy can be very helpful in promoting understanding between and among peoples.

Finally, the cognitive shift by African-Americans, gays, lesbians, women, Vietnam Veterans and other groups is an important illustration that cognitive change can make a real difference in people's lives.

3. Albert Ellis and Rational-Emotive Behavioral Therapy

Examination of case or presentation of videotape or film. I like to begin with a case illustration of Ellis. Gay and lesbian students have told me that they have particularly benefited from Epictetus and the Ellis framework. The process of "coming out" is a clear cognitive shift which requires emotional change. The ABCDEF framework can be helpful to move clients to a new view of self-in-system. A careful examination of the case in the chapter is one way to begin the presentation on Ellis.

Another way, of course, is to present an audiotape or videotape of Ellis in action. Specifically, I strongly recommend *against* the Gloria film. It is not a fair presentation of the current work that Ellis does and, as Ellis himself as noted wryly, the Gloria film tends to turn many students away from serious consideration of Ellis's important work.

I pay particular attention to the issue of style and the concept of authenticity. Ellis' New York style is not comfortable to all students. They may equate his style as the theory. I like to stress that you can do rational disputation in a very warm and supportive fashion in your own authentic style.

Lecture on main concepts. I like to start with how to identify irrational statements. I often assign homework in which students listen for irrational statements in their home environments. They are often amazed at how irrational the world is when one listens from Ellis' frame of reference. These observations can serve as a foundation for the ABCDEF constructs which follow.

Rational-Emotive Behavioral Therapy Self-Help Form. A live demonstration is helpful to the students here. I like to take the form in my hand, explain it to a volunteer from the class and then we work through the form together as an REBT therapist might in an actual session. Students seem to be reassured when they see me in an egalitarian way with the volunteer client as the two of work through the form. This experience takes away much of the hierarchical "feel" of REBT. The demonstration also helps students get a real understanding of how to work through the ABCDEF sequence.

Small group practice. I then divide the students into groups and they practice working on the form themselves in microskills-type practice sessions.

Issues of Alcoholism. At this point in the course, I like to stop and focus on alcohol issues, both from a Rational Recovery and an AA 12-step frame. While Ellis obviously prefers RR, it is helpful for students to realize that much of AA can be framed in cognitive-behavioral terms. I may bring in an AA speaker or show one of the valuable AA videotapes.

For homework, I ask students to visit an open meeting of AA or another alcohol self-help group. I also ask them to write up their own approach to this critical area stating that all of us need to have a conception of how we are going to consider alcoholism in our treatment and how we are going to work with AA and similar groups.

Aaron Beck and Cognitive Therapy

Review of case presentation. I have several audiotapes of Beck at work with depression, agoraphobia, and other clinical cases. I like to start by listening to one of these tapes with the students so that the clinical constructs come "live" to the class. Alternatively, a careful study of the case presentation on depression may be utilized to make the same points.

Groupwork on faulty thought patterns. It is useful to compare and contrast Beck's faulty thoughts with Ellis' irrational thoughts. Clearly, both look for cognitive style issues. I find that Ellis tends to work more directly and concretely with single issues of irrational ideas while Beck seems to be a bit more formal operational with his emphasis on patterns. But, both work at concrete and formal levels.

I like to list Ellis' system on the board and then put Beck's system beside it. Students are divided into groups and focus on similarities and differences between the two. I like to stress perfectionism as an underlying construct under many irrational ideas and faulty thoughts.

Automatic thoughts. I always have my students do homework in which they take a volunteer role-played clients through an automatic thoughts inventory. I also have them do a multicultural examination of the issues raised with the client. I sometimes do a live demonstration of the process. Students typically find this one of the more helpful exercises of the course. Too often students bypass this important technique without understanding its power and value.

Images and regression. On several of my audiotapes, Beck uses images much as described in the text. Beck uses images to draw out old experiences and then connect the old experience with present behavior. This is, of course, very similar to sensorimotor imaging within DCT and the imaging exercises of the psychodynamic chapter. By this point in the course, my students are very familiar with images and imagery exercises. At this point, we seem able to go into some depth into issues of regression around trauma.

I like to point out that Mary Bradford Ivey and I have used such techniques with children to good effect. Beck's techniques are highly adaptable to children as are those of Ellis and Glasser.

4. William Glasser and Reality Therapy

Introductory lecture. The same general format as above for Beck and Ellis can be followed for reality therapy. What I find most important is the word "responsibility" which Glasser seems to substitute for irrationality. The logical consequences portion of Glasser seems to me very similar to the A-B-C analysis of Ellis, but the word responsibility becomes the cognitive focus—and responsibility to live with the consequences of your actions.

I also like the hard, "real world" emphasis of Glasser, who seems to emphasize action more than Ellis and Beck. Glasser is very concrete and I think this is one of the reasons he is often more useful with teens and difficult populations than the other two authors.

Anyway, when students have mastered Ellis and Beck, they can easily master Glasser by changing their language, becoming a bit more concrete, and emphasizing consequences in the real world.

It is important to spend some time on control theory as part of Glasser's more recent thinking. I like to emphasize the idea of positive addictions and we spend a fair amount of class time on this concept, applying it to our own lives. The idea of positive addictions is very close to some of the ideas of Frankl and Lucas when they stress the importance of finding positive meanings in one's life.

Exercise in Cognitive-Behavior Therapy. The practice exercise on facing reality is good for in-class practice or for a homework assignment. In this case, focus on responsibility and the logical consequences of one's actions. Control theory can be used to analyze the interaction of the client with the world. We have worked rather hard on this particular exercise as we find it important in helping students and professionals make logical connections between CBT and multicultural theory.

Emphasis on youth. We tend to spend too much time on adults in our training. I like to bring in someone who is working directly with children or adolescents and have them talk about "what works." If you have a practicing reality therapist available, so much the better, but what is most important to me is to help my students realize that we need to adapt our techniques and strategies for work with younger populations.

5. Lazarus and the BASIC-ID.

I find it helpful to provide the students with a case for discussion. Their task is to identify the various aspects of the BASIC-ID and then to develop a treatment plan using these various issues. This seems to provide a very useful outline and summary of the CBT chapters. Moreover, it helps students generate ways to bring in other chapters in the text as well.

The exercise presented is useful in helping them transfer ideas from the class and text to actual practice.

6. But, what about multicultural issues? At this point in the course, I like to return to MCT, Paulo Freire, and cultural identity theory. I like to point out that cognitive change is critical in MCT work, but the cognitions there also focus on contextual issues. I've found it highly valuable to set of teams of students who compare and contrast MCT theory and cognitive theories of Beck, Ellis, Lazarus, and Glasser. Each of the teams is to report back on how they might integrate MCT with these traditional cognitive theorists.

Recall that Freire seeks to help people move to new cognitive understandings of themselves in relation to oppressive systems. Ellis' ABC analysis, Beck's automatic thoughts, the BASIC-ID of Lazarus, and Glasser's concepts of responsibility are all quite adaptable to and MCT orientation. Similarly, I believe traditional theories presented in this chapter might be more effective if focus were placed on the family and multicultural issues.

Multiple Choice Questions

Associate each of the following concepts with the appropriate cognitive theorist:

1. Irrational ideas
   a) Aaron Beck
   b) Arnold Lazarus
   c) Albert Ellis*
   d) William Glasser

2. Automatic thoughts
   a) Aaron Beck*
   b) Arnold Lazarus
   c) Albert Ellis
   d) William Glasser

3. *Conscientizacào*

   a) Aaron Beck
   b) Paulo Freire*
   c) Albert Ellis
   d) William Glasser

4. Control theory

   a) Aaron Beck
   b) Arnold Lazarus

c) Albert Ellis
d) William Glasser*

5. Consciousness raising

a) Aaron Beck
b) Paulo Freire*
c) Albert Ellis
d) William Glasser

6. Imagery and regression

a) Aaron Beck*
b) Arnold Lazarus
c) Albert Ellis
d) William Glasser

7. Responsibility

a) Aaron Beck
b) Paulo Freire
c) Albert Ellis
d) William Glasser*

8. Strong in cultural aspects of cognition

a) Aaron Beck
b) Paulo Freire*
c) Albert Ellis
d) William Glasser

9. Integrative theory

a) Aaron Beck
b) Arnold Lazarus*
c) Albert Ellis
d) William Glasser

10. Which of the following is most often associated with the cognitive tradition?

a) Correct thought manifest themselves in correct action.
b) We are not disturbed by events, but by our view of them.*
c) To thine own self be true.
d) Associate with good colleagues and you will good thoughts.

11 Multicultural authorities criticize the cognitive theorists because

a) these techniques were created by White males.

b) women's perceptions have been minimized and misunderstood.*
c) conscious and unconscious racism by many practitioners.
d) the techniques are less than useful with African-American and Mexican-American clients.

12. In looking at cognitive theory, the text comments

a) feminist issues are incompatible with the cognitive orientation.
b) with adaptation, all cognitive techniques are useful for multicultural populations.
c) the Black identity movement has done more for African-American mental health than all counseling theories combined.*
d) cognitive therapy is rapidly moving toward cultural awareness.

13. The text cites him as "very likely the first person in the CBT movement who included multicultural cognitive issues as an explicit part of the treatment process."

a) Paul Freire
b) Harold Cheatham
c) Albert Ellis
d) Donald Cheek*

14. Rational disputation is an important part of the theories of

a) Beck and Ellis*
b) Cheek and Ellis
c) Cheek and Beck
d) Glasser and Ellis

15. REBT seeks to

a) help clients examine their lives.
b) cure client thinking patterns.
c) help clients examine their illogical thought processes.*
d) challenge client behavior which is ineffective.

16. Which theorist has focused most on issues of alcoholism?

a) Aaron Beck
b) Arnold Lazarus
c) Albert Ellis*
d) William Glasser

17. Relationship between client and therapist

a) is less important in the cognitive approaches than other theories as thinking takes such an important part.
b) is important to Beck and Glasser, but not to Ellis.

c) is examined constantly in the cognitive tradition.
d) remains foundational in cognitive theory.*

18. Meta-analysis of Beck's cognitive therapy reveals

a) it is more effective than Ellis' work.
b) that it is more effective than medication.*
c) it is more effective than Glasser's work.
d) all of the above.

19. Meta-analysis of REBT reminds us

a) clients who experience this type of therapy appear to benefit.*
b) it is the most effective form of cognitive therapy.
c) other forms of cognitive therapy are more effective.
d) a and b above.

20. Which theorist tends to be the most formal operational, emphasizing patterns?

a) Aaron Beck*
b) Arnold Lazarus
c) Albert Ellis
d) William Glasser

21. Concrete work in the "real world" is most often associated with

a) Aaron Beck
b) Arnold Lazarus
c) Albert Ellis
d) William Glasser*

22. The daily record of automatic thoughts is

a) a useful mental health exercise for us all.
b) specifically helpful for depressed patients.
c) a neat way to understand our client's cognitive processes.
d) b and c above.
e) all of the above.*

23. Beck differs from Ellis in that

a) he pays little attention to past developmental history.
b) he often examines developmental history to understand present patterns of living.*
c) emotion is less emphasized and the focus is placed on automatic thoughts.
d) emotion is emphasized whereas REBT focuses more on rationality.

24. Which is most often associated with reality therapy?

a) careful attention to client thoughts.
b) emotional understanding.
c) consideration of consequences of one's actions.*
d) cognitive restructuring.

25. Glasser's control theory emphasizes

a) controlling one's emotions.
b) controlling one's cognitions.
c) owning thoughts, behavior, and feelings and being responsible for them.*
d) noting distinctions between and among thoughts, behaviors, and feelings for better control of self-understanding.

26. Positive addictions might include from Glasser's frame of reference

a) swimming, jogging, and nutrition.*
b) choosing our own ways of controlling our lives thus moving out of the addictive process.
c) joining a relapse prevention group.
d) becoming more attuned to multicultural issues and problems.

27. According to the text, regression techniques should be

a) avoided due to the danger of implanting your experience in the client's head.
b) a treatment of choice when working with complex issues.
c) a useful supplement to Shapiro's work in eye movement desensitization and reprocessing.
d) used with care and with clear cooperation from the client.*

28. Missing from Lazarus' BASIC-ID is

a) multicultural issues.*
b) the importance of drugs and health matters.
c) interpersonal relationships.
d) sensations.

Essay Questions

1. A client comes to you stating that he "only" made an 85 on his last examination and wants help from you so that he can study more effectively. On listening more closely to his story, you discover that 85 was the top mark the professor gave. The student insists that he must make at least 90 on paper. How would you conduct an Ellis ABC analysis of this client's cognitions? How would you treat using the DEF concepts?

2. Compare and contrast Ellis and Beck's approach to cognitive therapy.

3. How is Glasser a cognitive theorist? How is he similar to and how is he different from Ellis?

4. Present a multicultural critique of cognitive therapy. What are this methods strengths and weaknesses when viewed from an MCT perspective?

5. Outline the main points of Ellis (or Beck or Glasser) and provide a multicultural evaluation of each of these points.

6. Outline the major points of the BASIC-ID and how they are helpful in case conceptualization.

SUGGESTED SUPPLEMENTARY READING

Beck, A., and Freeman, A. *Cognitive Therapy of Personality Disorders.* New York: Guilford, 1990.

> Beck's recent with personality disorders is highly informative and practical. The ideas presented here are quite compatible with the model presented in this book on psychodynamic case conceptualization.

Beck, A., J. Rush, Shaw, B., Emery, G. *Cognitive Therapy of Depression.* New York: Guilford, 1980.

> One of the classic works of the cognitive-behavioral movement. A variety of cognitively-oriented techniques to facilitate planning and thinking in dealing with depression.

Ellis, A. *Growth Through Reason: Verbatim Cases in Rational-Emotive Therapy.* Palo Alto, CA: Science and Behavior Books, 1971.

> A particular strength of REBT has been a constant emphasis on clarifying what therapists of this persuasion actually do to help people. The typescripts in this book are carefully analyzed and interestingly presented.

Ellis, A. (1994) *Reason and Emotion in Psychotherapy.* New York: Birch Lane.

> One of Ellis' most impressive accomplishments is his ability to change and grow. This book outlines the reasons he moved from RET to REBT. Ellis in his usual, lucid presentation provides a strong statement on his belief system and ideas about therapy and counseling.

Trimpey, J. *Rational Recovery from Addiction: The Small Book.* Lotus, Ca: Author, 1990

It is vital that all counselors and therapists have an understanding of the addictive process and Alcoholics Anonymous. This book will provide a useful supplement from an REBT frame of reference.

Glasser, W. *Reality Therapy.* New York: Harper & Row, 1965.

The original statement on reality therapy which came to wide national attention. The book is a useful overview of philosophy and method.

Glasser, W. *Take Effective Control of Your Life.* New York: Harper and Row, 1984.

Glasser's most recent statement of his developing position. Here you will find increasing parallels with the cognitive-behavioral position. Several practical suggestions for daily living are contained in this book written for the popular market.

Lazarus, A. (1992) *I Can if I Want To.* New York: Murrow.

A popularized version of multimodal therapy. Useful to beginners and as a supplementary handout for clients if one is conducting cognitive-behavioral therapy.

Chapter 11

The Existential-Humanistic Tradition I: Existential-Humanistic Theory and Person-Centered Theory

Overview

This chapter starts with an introduction to the philosophic background of the existential-humanistic tradition followed by an in-depth and practical presentation of the work of Carl Rogers. Students should complete this chapter with an understanding of basic philosophy and the ability to engage in person-centered-type counseling and therapy, at least in a beginning form. In addition, new material from Clemmont Vontress will open up spirituality and counseling in a challenging way. This text has taken a small risk in presenting spirituality as so important a part of therapy, but our reading of the literature is that this concepts is very much going to be part of our future.

This chapter is structured as follows:

- The Existential-Humanistic Worldview
  - Being-in-the-World
  - Existential Commitment, Intentionality, and the I-Thou Relationship
  - Multicultural Issues

- The Rogerian Revolution
  - Adding Multicultural Dimensions to Self-Actualization Theory
  - The Influence of Rogers
  - Case Examples from Three Periods of Rogers' Work
    - The Nondirective Period
    - The Client-Centered Period
    - The Person-Centered Period
  - Central Theoretical Constructs and Techniques
- Limitations and Practical Implications of the Existential-Humanistic Tradition.

The aim of the chapter is to present a general philosophic structure and then to present Carl Rogers' work as an implementation of that philosophy. Rogers' influence on the field has been immense and we must recall that the facilitative conditions (Chapter 2) and the listening portion of the microskills framework (Chapter 3) were derived from his seminal thinking.

A major effort in this chapter is to point out how Rogers' thinking constantly evolved over time. He was always changing and growing and thus provides an exceptionally good personal model for all of us at this time of change in our own field. The chapter is written to suggest that Rogers would likely be supportive of today's multicultural emphasis.

Class Procedures

1. The Existential-Humanistic Worldview and Multicultural Implications. I tend to present this material in lecture format. I tend to repeat the material presented and amplify it according to the experiential level of the class. With undergrads, I tend to explain what is there, with grads I add more material as time permits.

A Play Reading. I particularly like to present Sartre's play *No Exit* and have students conduct a play reading in front of class. Then, I ask students to define key existential constructs such as anxiety, commitment, and intentionality as they manifest themselves in characters in the play. From this experience, existential concepts become real rather than abstract.

Finally, the Eurocentric orientation of the play and the existential-humanistic concepts can be considered. These ideas are very individualistic, although they point to the importance of relationship. Students could be encouraged to generate a new construction of this philosophic orientation with a more comprehensive multicultural perspective.

2. Self-Actualization: Multicultural Critique. Using the eigenwelt, mitwelt, and umwelt constructs coupled with the microskill of focus, students can examine the multicultural debate around this concept. The concept of self-in-relation is compatible with Rogers. I believe Rogers was moving in the direct of self-in-relation at the time of his death, but many of his adherents pay insufficient attention to his final work on issues of peace and world understanding.

Rigney points out that in many traditional cultures, the Maslow hierarchy of needs in totally inappropriate. "Placing self-actualization at the top of the so-called hierarchy is simply incorrect for my people. We are who we are because of our relations with the group." Rigney's direct challenge to Maslow and self-actualization ("That word seems selfish to me.") illustrates that even the fabled Rogers and Maslow are subject to multicultural criticism.

3. Rogers' Influence. Despite the possible criticisms above, let us recall that Rogers has had immense influence throughout the world in many cultures. He is often the first counselor or therapist that trainee's hear of. In some ways, his influence is more extensive than Freud's.

Particularly, I like to point out to my students that behavioral therapy had to change and become more relationship-oriented due to criticism from the person-centered theorists. Similarly, Rogers has forced psychodynamic and other orientations to look much more closely at relationship issues.

Given this, I think Rogers would respond in some very healthy, positive, and supportive ways to today's multicultural and gender challenges. Nonetheless, this would suggest that he theories need to be updated as time passes and we learn more about the change process.

4. View Rogers in Action. Nothing seems better to present Rogers to students than a film or videotape. I still like to show the old Gloria tapes and he comes across very positively to most students.

However, we all need to be aware that the Gloria tapes and a considerable amount of Rogers' work was highly individualistic. I now find it necessary to point out to my students that they will find old, sexist behaviors in the Gloria film. I tell them that after the film that they will be asked to do a multicultural, gender critique of what they see.

5. Practice Rogerian Counseling. I like to ask students in class to do an interview using only listening skills as presented in practice exercises. In my sequencing, I like to present Rogers' work along with Chapters 2 and 3 as a unit.

6. Transferental Issues in Rogerian Counseling. Weinrach's article is an important historical contribution to our field. There you will find the missing 249 words and you can make your own decision in the Weinrach-Bohart debate on transference. Weinrach would be glad to share a reprint of his article. Write for a reprint to:

Stephen G. Weinrach, Ph.D.
2110 Darby Creek Broad
Havertown, PA 19083

Students find the debate fascinating and feel a part of the development of the field as they consider the issues.

7. Vontress, Spirituality, and Multicultural Issues. The *Uberwelt* concept needs to be explored in some depth as it has not received full recognition in our field. Students will need some time to process and discuss the issues of religion and spirituality as they apply to counseling and therapy. I have found that many beginning counselors are surprised that the issue has not been considered in real depth by our field.

In addition, Vontress' comments on the matter of stress and its effects on the immune system need special consideration. It is becoming clearer year by year that meaning issues affect bodily functioning. Spirituality and existential-humanistic approaches speak to these issues with some clarity.

The exercise on the meaning of being in the world is new to this edition and provides a structured way to make the oft-times vague ideas of existential-humanistic thought more specific and useable to beginning counselors and therapists.

Multiple Choice Questions

1. The person and her or his body.

   a) eigenwelt*
   b) mitwelt
   c) umwelt
   d) Uberwelt

2. According to existential thought, any attempt to separate ourselves from the world results involves

   a) eigenwelt.
   b) binswanger welt.
   c) alienation.*
   d) anxiety.

3. The biological and physical world

   a) eigenwelt
   b) mitwelt
   c) umwelt*
   d) Uberwelt

4. A feminist critique of the existential-humanistic tradition might be:

   a) there are no women theorists associated prominently with this tradition.
   b) the intense focus on the individual is incompatible with a more environmentally-oriented approach.
   c) the concepts are irrelevant to women.
   d) and b above.*
   e) all of the above

5. Self-actualization implies focusing

   a) on the individual.*
   b) on self-in-relation.
   c) on network therapy.
   d) on eigenwelt, umwelt, and mitwelt issues.

6. "You're feeling overwhelmed by your marriage. You just don't know what to do." This counseling lead focuses on

a) eigenwelt.*
b) mitwelt.
c) umwelt.
d) self-in-relation.

7. "The world seems a very confusing place. War, trauma, racism." This counseling lead focuses on

a) eigenwelt.*
b) mitwelt.
c) umwelt.*
d) Uberwelt.

8. "You and Jonnie are having a difficult time. You're wondering how to work it out more successfully.

a) eigenwelt.
b) mitwelt.*
c) umwelt.
d) self-in-relation.* (two answers possible)

9. Research on person-centered theory reveals

a) it is the most effective type of therapy.
b) that these type of therapists are the most warm and caring.
c) that experts of all theoretical orientations show more effective relationship skills than inexperienced therapists.*
d) a and b above.
e) all of the above.

10. An emphasis on listening skills and client's finding their own direction is characteristic of Rogers'

a) non-directive period.*
b) self-actualization period.
c) client-centered period.
d) person-centered period.

11. Increased emphasis on groupwork and issues such as world peace is characteristic of Rogers'

a) non-directive period.
b) self-actualization period.
c) client-centered period.
d) person-centered period.*

12. Rogers is known for his ability to focus on

a) the network of relationships.

b) gender issues.
c) the individual*
d) the family.

13. Rogers' view of transference is that

a) an unneeded construct.*
b) a vital part of understanding therapeutic process.
c) it is critical to understand as part of the self-actualization process.
d) is a central construct to all helping theories.

14. Rogers' work is closely associated with what portion of the microskills framework?

a) listening skills*
b) influencing skills
c) focusing skills
d) self-in-relation skills

15. Person-centered theory assumes

a) people hold many irrational ideas.
b) dreams are important to understand the human condition.
c) people are forward moving and self-actualizing.*
d) the human condition is too complex to understand, so we need to center our focus on the person.

16. Person-centered strongly emphasizes

a) the importance of listening to client's perceptions of events.
b) the value of diagnosis through listening.
c) the importance of relationship.
d) a and c above.*
e. all of the above.

17. Empathy is a construct underlying most counseling practice today. Which theorist had the most influence in leading us in this direction?

a) Freud
b) Skinner
c) Meichenbaum
c) Rogers*

18. Rogers ended his working career by

a) developing new ways to run encounter groups.
b) severely criticizing the psychodynamic fame of reference.
c) changing his frame of reference about multicultural issues.

d) working toward world peace.*

19. Rogers was the first prominent therapist to

a) criticize psychodynamic theory in an effective way that led to change.
b) emphasize the importance of the individual.
c) stress the role of emotion in the session.
d) open his work to the critique of others through presenting transcripts and tapes of his sessions.*

20. The Gloria films, according to Weinrach and Beaver,

a) illustrate a positive way to conduct therapy.
b) have had immense influence for positive change.
c) exemplify transference and lack of sensitivity to gender issues.*
d) a and b above.

21. Vontress adds special attention to which two dimensions of existential-humanistic thought?

a) eigenwelt and mitwelt
b) mitwelt and umwelt
c) eigenwelt and Uberwelt
d) umwelt and Uberwelt

22. A spiritual orientation to therapy, according to Vontress

a) is essential to a full understanding of the individual.*
b) must be approached with care as the ideas as new and untested.
c) is in clear opposition to the Rogerian client-centered tradition.
d) requires that we be of the same spiritual orientation as our client.

23. Self-actualization can be enriched, according to the text, by

a) awareness of self-in-relation.
b) multicultural inclusion.
c) spiritual dimensions.
d) a and c above.
e) all of the above.

Essay Questions

1. Rogers has been criticized for his excessive emphasis on the individual and the failure to consider contextual, gender issues. What is the nature

of this critique and how might his theory be adapted to meet these new challenges?

2. Define the essence of Roger's three periods of development as defined by the text. Imagine he were still alive today. What might a fourth period look like?

3. How do the facilitative conditions of Chapter 2 and the microskills of Chapter 3 relate to Rogers' work?

4. The Gloria films have had immense influence on the field. What has been the extent of this influence and what are some current issues regarding these important films? Define your own position in the current controversy.

5. Imagine that a client approaches you asking for help in "coming out" as a gay or lesbian person. Compare and contrast the approaches of Albert Ellis and Carl Rogers to this client.

6. Spirituality has been presented by Vontress as an important dimension in counseling and therapy. What is your position on Vontress' ideas? How would you implement your position in counseling and therapy?

SUGGESTED SUPPLEMENTARY READING

Buber, M. *I and Thou*. New York: Scribner's, 1970.

> This book might be described as the ``heart" of the existential-humanistic tradition. Buber discusses the nature of the human condition and relationship in poetic terms.

May, R., E. Angel, and H. Ellenberger. *Existence.* New York: Simon & Schuster, 1958.

> A basic text covering readings by prominent existential authors such as May, Minkowski, and Binswanger.

Rogers, C. *On Becoming a Person*. Boston: Houghton-Mifflin, 1961.

> Rogers' best known and classic work. The exposition of method and philosophy is exceptionally clear and well drawn. This book becomes a treasure to many students.

Rogers, C. *On Encounter Groups.* New York: Harper & Row, 1970.

> This book illustrates how much a person can change over a period of ten years. Rogers moved from a prime interest in counseling and

psychotherapy to a deep commitment to group work over that time. The descriptions of group process are particularly lucid. It remains one of the best descriptions of group process ever written.

Sartre, J. *No Exit.* New York: Knopf, 1946.

Existentialism as a philosophy becomes complex with a wide and varied vocabulary. Literature such as *No Exit* is often better at describing existentialism. Sartre has a special gift for presenting the human condition—what exists exists. *No Exit* is a play that describes the existential problems of three people committed to hell, which is represented as a single room from which they are unable to leave. The analogies to everyday life experience are implicit but clear.

Vontress, C. (1986) Social and cultural foundations. In M. Lewis, R. Hayes, and J. Lewis, An Introduction to the Counseling Profession. Itasca, IL: Peacock.

A general statement of Vontress's position.

Chapter 12

The Existential-Humanistic Tradition: Logotherapy and Experiential Gestalt Therapy

Overview

Viktor Frankl is an encompassing theorist who represents the highest ideals of the existential-humanistic tradition. He is recognized as an important originator of the cognitive movement, met directly with Freud, and he has wide multicultural appeal. Due to his breadth and the excellent applied and theoretical work of his student/colleague Elisabeth Lukas, his work will likely have increased influence as the years come.

To be honest, Frankl is a hero to me. His book *Man's Search for Meaning* has made a difference in my life and that of my family. I have known many people who find their suffering bearable due to this one book. I could not recommend it more highly.

In my three meetings with Frankl and working with him on this chapter, he has impressed me with his scholarship and commitment to his ideals. However, even more so, I have been impressed by his passion for life, his absolute faith in the individual, and his energy and vitality when I last talked with him at the age of 85. He does not come across as the warm, caring Rogers, but rather as the impressive, dignified German professor. He commands respect and gets it.

This chapter presents Frankl as one of the most complete theorists we have available, yet we must recall that his presentation focuses very much on the Eurocentric individualistic tradition. Of necessity, in the concentration camp, we find Frankl emphasizing how individuals make meaning and survive impossible situations. While relationships were important, to me his theory is extremely individualistic, giving relatively little attention to contextual/environmental issues. Nonetheless, I believe there is room for expansion of his ideas into environmental action.

And, we need to recall that his experience surviving the holocaust is a model of meaning for all oppressed people.

Fritz Perls, I like for very different reasons. I never met him, but was fortunate enough to watch him work at the famous Washington APA meetings. His demands and expectations on the client, his skill in front of an audience, and his charisma were amazing to me. I found him refreshingly honest about the human condition. This chapter attempts to catch some of the essence of a legendary figure. It is sad that he died before his community work on Vancouver Island reached any meaningful conclusions.

For Frankl, this chapter presents selections from *Man's Search for Meaning,* the central theoretical constructs and techniques of logotherapy, and it multicultural implications.

For Perls, this chapter focuses on a case example and specific techniques of his work. The theories undergirding his frame of reference are interesting, but have had minimal influence on the field His techniques are likely to be his lasting contribution.

As you can sense, I can't imagine any therapist or counselor as being complete without some contact with these two giants. (But, then that holds true in terms in my admiration for Freud, Bowlby, Attneave, Freire, Jackson, Rogers, and other key authors cited in this book.)

Classroom Procedures

1. *Man's Search for Meaning.* This book is a superb supplemental reading. It is brief and students always enjoy and get something important out of the experience. And, they have a therapeutic resource for their clients immediately in hand. I simply start this class by dividing into groups and asking them to share their experience of the book. We then debrief the experience in class and outline the key ideas which come out of the book and their experience.

If you do not assign the book, the brief material on Frankl's life may be sufficient. Students can also share their own experience and observations on the importance of meaning making.

Multicultural extensions. It is helpful to focus on oppressed groups and how they make meaning for survival. When dealing with racism, childhood oppression, homophobia, and other forms of discrimination, one important mode of survival is transcending the horrors one must endure almost daily. "It is not events, but how we view events." It is a challenge to extend Frankl's thinking to this area, but it is a profitable class exercise and one that can have lasting influence on their thinking and practice. At the same time, the meaning-making process must not substitute for action against oppression.

2. Frankl' s techniques. At this point in the course, I like to use student expertise. I divide the students into groups and ask them to plan a demonstration themselves of the major techniques offered by Frankl. This helps concretize the work for the students.

3. Modification of Attitudes: An Interview Example Following is an interview example focusing on modification of attitudes. Some terms, I pass out this interview and we analyze it as a way to integrate theories, while focusing on changing cognitive attitudes as suggested by Frankl. In effect, the following interview is a gentle disputation of irrational ideas and the purpose is to change thinking and cognition.

Permission to copy this interview is granted for classroom purposes.

This is the third demonstration session between therapist Mary and client Charles. In this interview Mary emphasizes a version of Frankl's system of finding positive meanings or ``modification of attitudes.'' Note that the counselor is able to facilitate client development of a new view of the situation primarily using microskills of listening. For the most part, she uses the client's main words as he seeks to reinterpret and look at a past situation more positively. You will also note the use of sensorimotor experiencing and some techniques similar to that of the psychodynamic orientation. The repetition is characteristic of Gestalt therapy.

The goal of modification of attitudes is cognitive change through reframing or reinterpreting the meaning of old situations.

1.M: I'm going to demonstrate the positive asset search and hunt for more positive meanings in a manner somewhat parallel to those of Frankl. To start this Charles, I'd like to have you move to your shoulders and get with the feeling of the kinds of things we've been talking about.
Information/Directive

2.C: Yeah, OK . . . (closes eyes, hands reach to shoulders as if to take on even more responsibility. Mary waits and watches closely).

3.M: Can you feel it even more?
Directive

3.C: (Sigh) . . . Yeah
(The client moves into the experience more deeply. He is moving toward deep concentration on the feelings. Mary knows from experience that this client is predominately kinesthetic and thus works directly with the feeling perceptual system. With most clients, you will find a deeper emotional experience with the kinesthetic dimensions than with auditory or visual.)

5.M: Umm-hum . . . umm-hum . . .
Encourager

6.C: OK.
(From observation of his nonverbals, Mary knows that the client has entered into emotions fairly fully.)

7.M: Can you go back to a childhood experience or an earlier situation where you felt this heaviness on your shoulders? Can you talk a little bit about it?
Directive phrased as closed question

(This is the psychodynamic focused free association technique.)

8.C: Oh . . . I was about, about nine, and a friend and I were out--we trespassed on somebody else's property and we were . . . ah . . . pushing logs along a kind of slough or stream. And it was great fun, playing around in the water and just really fun. I didn't quite feel comfortable being there, but . . .

9.M: So it was fun, but not exactly comfortable.
Reflection of feeling/confrontation
(This is a confrontation because Mary has selected out the mixed emotions expressed by the client. It is the ambivalent or mixed feelings that are often most important in counseling and therapy.)

10.C: Well it . . . (pause) . . . you've got it. And then I--we went to cross a cow path and I got stuck and we couldn't move.

11.M: Stuck in the path?
Encourager

12.C: And, something like--kind of quicksand because I started to go down deeper. . . . I don't know what really would have happened . . . if it really was quicksand. I was convinced I was going to die. And there we were, where we didn't belong and I couldn't get out. Very, very scary.

13.M: So you were feeling very scary and just sinking down?
Reflection of feeling and paraphrase

14.C: Yeah, I just shouldn't have been there. I shouldn't have been there. And I said this is what happens when I don't do the right thing. Ah, I get some of those same feelings of fear in my stomach right now . . . ah . . .

(At this point, the client is experiencing present-tense immediacy--reliving the past in the present.)

15.M: So fear and feeling you're going to die, very, very afraid.
Reflection of feeling

16.C: And Jerry tried to dig me out and he couldn't. So then I really got scared. And then Jerry left and I was there all by myself, and nothing I could do. And then, Jerry came back with Mr. Olson, and . . . ah, he yelled at me and he dug me out and everything was OK and I went home. But, I remember I washed my boots off and I wouldn't tell anyone about it and I just felt terribly guilty and it really was something that I shouldn't have done. I just never, we were talking, I just felt--you know--really that I should stay away from other people's space and take care of myself and, you know, in that situation.

(There are some interesting cultural aspects to this description. Note that the client is still assuming internal responsibility for a childhood event. The word ``guilt'' is highly characteristic of European-American middle-class youth from his cultural background. You will also note that he takes individual responsibility for his actions and says nothing about the friend who was with him. Other cultural groups might consider playing in this way a ``right'' and would not have to wash off their boots to ``remove'' the guilt.)

17.M: So you had all kinds of feelings associated with this early childhood experience, including, you know, feeling like you shouldn't be doing this . . . feeling guilty, feeling you're in somebody else's space--you shouldn't be there--lots of negative feelings I hear associated with that.
Summary

18.C: Oh God . . . yes . . .

19.M: Is there anything that comes to mind that's positive? I know it sounds like a totally negative experience. Was there anything that you could see that was positive about what happened?
Open question oriented to finding positive meanings

(The positive asset search (modification of attitudes) begins here. Mary has listened to the client carefully and now starts to search out positives in the situation. Verbal clients, experienced in therapy, are likely to respond quickly and easily to this direct approach. Other clients may respond more slowly; or they may prefer one of the several alternative routes toward finding positives in negatives.)

20.C: . . . (pause) . . . Well, it sure felt good when he dug me out. I was scared, but felt guilty, but he at least dug me out.

21.M: So you felt like there was help even though you were afraid and . .
Reflection of feeling

22.C: And you know what? Jerry, you know, really tried to help me and he went and got Mr. Olson. And, ah . . . I was afraid of Mr. Olson after that?

23.M: So, it made you think that you had friends there if you were in trouble.
Interpretation

24.C: . . . Well, I didn't really feel that I had friends . . . but, if I start thinking about it, it really does. I did have friends. And then actually, Mr. Olson then called next week and asked me to work for him on his farm. . . . I think I've always paid attention to the negative part of that experience. . . . It really was . . . there were people there.

25.M: There were people to help in difficult situations like that.
Encourager/Restatement

26.C: Yes, yes . . .

27.M: And Mr. Olson even didn't really blame you for it. In fact, he even . . . ah . . . called and hired you to do other work for him later on.
Paraphrase

28.C: I didn't have to take as much on my shoulders as I thought I did.

(This is a particularly important and interesting comment on part of the client. He reinterprets the old situation from a new, more positive frame of reference. He has generated a new perspective on the situation himself with the aid of the therapist. This new view, interestingly, is less self-centered and more relational in nature. Note that Mary has been using listening skills almost exclusively.)

29.M: Didn't need as much. Well, how does this relate to all these other problems we've been talking about with your secretary and with the kids? If there is any relationship between the two? Do you see any patterns?
Encourager/open question/confrontation

(The client had earlier stated a problem in taking on too much responsibility for the behavior of his children and for his secretary, often getting himself in trouble due to failure to maintain adequate boundaries. The therapist here searches for repeating patterns and asks the client to examine the old situation from childhood to determine if there are residues in daily life now. The confrontation involves the comparison of the past situation with the present issues- a formal operational process).

30.C: Well, the thing that stood out from the first session, Mary, was me being more nurturing and responsible than I needed to be. (M: Umm-humm, Umm-humm.) . . . Ahh, and in effect, that's almost like taking more on my shoulders than I need to. And, in one situation back as a kid, I had those feelings of fear. But, now I have these feelings of anger . . . and, you know, somehow I know fear and anger go together.

31.M: How do they go together?
Open question

32.C: I don't really understand fully, but I know that somehow they are close together, so that's something we need to explore more later . . . more deeply . . .

33.M: Sounds like a pattern, though, of taking on too much responsibility, whether its . . .
Interpretation

34.C: Whether it's Georgia, the kids . . . or Mr. Olsen . . . sometimes I get angry, other times scared. We've got something for next time.

35.M: So, today, we've looked at a scary situation from way back and we find that even in negative situations there are positives. Perhaps that will give us a clue for the next session.

Summary

In this case, modification of attitudes has helped the client, Charles, find a new meaning in an old situation. Metaphorically, Charles was trapped in a prison of negative meanings in the situation. With the aid of the therapist, he was able to reconstrue his perceptions of the world and modify his attitudes in a more positive way. Theory holds that this new perception of events will stay with the client and gradually help him to look at new situations, as well, more positively. His worldview has been challenged and a beginning toward change has been made.

The therapist's use of microskills in this last session is particularly effective. She brings out the facts, feelings, and underlying meanings that the client has toward the event and enables the client intentionally to generate new meanings. Mary, the therapist, has shown good individual empathy; being sensitive, she is culturally appropriate as well. Nonetheless, the counselor has assumed individualistically oriented therapy is appropriate. The same methods might not be as successful if the client came from a different cultural background.

4. Perls and a Case Example. A film of Perls may be presented. I am not fond of the Gloria film of Perls as he really didn't use his more famous techniques at that point. At this point, I still haven't found a Perls' film I like. If you know of one, please let me know.

So, at present I tend to use material available on transcript on Perls and we examine his style. The interview from the book is a good representative example of his work. A live Gestalt dream analysis demonstration helps the techniques believable and useful to the class.

5. Personal Experience with Gestalt. About twenty years ago, I found myself starting to develop a phobia around flying. The anxiety started getting fairly high. Flying into Minneapolis, I felt the fear as we are starting to land. I then used Gestalt techniques on myself with the intention of finding the meaning of the airplane to me. As Fritz might do, I directed myself to say, "I am the airplane." and then see what happened. It came out something like this:

> "I am the airplane and I have Allen inside me and he's under my control and there's nothing he can do."

It may not sound like much, but it led me to say the next time I got on the airplane, "I am getting on the airplane, it's my decision and I'm in control." This little mantra was very helpful to me. I know it is irrational, but it worked. My fear of flying disappeared over the next three or four flights. Occasionally, I have the beginnings of a reoccurrence, but the mantra takes it away. Albert Ellis would not like this resolution, but it works for me.

I like to tell this story and then apply it to Gestalt dream analysis. Any number of times, I have woken up with dreams in the middle of the night that I wanted to understand. While psychodynamic free association is often helpful, more useful, I find, is "becoming" objects or people in the dream and using "I statements" as if I were that person or object in the dream and seeing what comes from the "I statement." Often useful learnings appear.

After this sharing, I have students do the same with some event or dream in their own life by themselves and then share with each other in small groups their experiences and observations.

6. Classroom Demonstrations of Gestalt Skills. Again, I like to divide the class into groups and they each demonstrate the various Gestalt skills and strategies.

7. The Getsmart Prayer. I like to put this on an overhead and ask students to share their reactions. It is from *Rough Times,* a now defunct journal of the late 60's and early 70's, but it speaks to multicultural issues and the Eurocentric nature of our traditional approach to helping.

> You do your thing, and
> I'll do my thing, and
> If by change we meet, it's beautiful.
>
> You are you and I am I.
> And if by chance we find
> Our brothers and sisters enslaved
> And the world under fascist rule
> Because we're doing out thing—
> It can't be helped.

Multiple Choice Questions

1. Frankl's emphasis on modifying the way we think about things places him close to:

   a) the psychodynamic tradition.
   b) the person-centered humanistic tradition

c) the cognitive tradition*
d) the multicultural tradition.

2. Finding positive meanings in impossible situations, we most often associate with

a) Carl Rogers.
b) Donald Meichenbaum.
c) Albert Ellis.
d) Viktor Frankl.*

3. Important in Frankl's modification of attitudes is

a) listening carefully to the client's construction of reality.
b) moving the client to behavioral action.
c) reframing attitudes.
d) a and c above
e) all of the above.*

4. The originator of paradoxical intention was

a) Frankl*
b) Perls
c) Erickson
d) Lukas

5. In paradoxical intention, we encourage clients to

a) exaggerate a symptom.
b) do the opposite of what they intend.
c) encourage the client to do the very things feared.*
d) a and c above.
e) all of the above.

6. Hyper-reflection occurs when clients

a) focus on negative attitudes.
b) focus on our feelings to the exclusion of cognitions.
c) think about ourselves and our problems excessively.
d) a and b above.
e) all of the above.*

7. Dereflection, as a technique of logotherapy emphasizes the importance of:

a) dereflecting on cognitions and refocusing on emotions.
b) thinking about something other than the problem.*
c) listening to the client's construction of reality.

d) a and b above.
e) all of the above.

8. Dereflection has been found especially useful for

a) sexual dysfunctioning.
b) insomnia.
c) a passive-aggressive personality style.
d) a and b above.*
e) all of the above.

9. The appealing technique is similar to what might happen in

a) Rational Recovery
b) Alcoholics Anonymous*
c) Cognitive orientations to alcohol recovery
d) all of the above.
e) none of the above.

10. Spirituality, Elisabeth Lukas holds

a) leads us to think beyond our Ego.*
b) can lead to living more in the moment peacefully.
c) helps us live more effectively in the past.
d) a difficult construct to integrate with the psychotherapy process.

11. Frankl argues that we need to make a decision for

a) the past.
b) the present.
c) the future.*
d) a and c above.
e) all of the above.

12. "Do your own thing" is characteristic of

a) the relational orientation.
b) the self-in-relation.
c) Latina/o culture.
d) individualistic perspectives.*

13. Perls saw humankind as

a) disordered and confused.
b) essentially positive and forward moving.
c) holistic, consisting of many parts that make the unique person.*
d) an integrated whole or Gestalt.

14. Microskill particularly characteristic of Gestalt therapy.

a) feedback
b) reflection of feeling
c) interpretation
d) directive*

15. In Perls later life, he

a) focused more deeply on individualistic perspectives.
b) became highly supportive of gender, multicultural interests.
c) developed an interest in community and extended Gestalt work to larger groups.*
d) returned to his earlier writings which focused on traditional Freudian perspectives

16. Enns talks of Gestalt's implications for women pointing out

a) that Perls was extremely sexist.
b) individualistic orientations of Gestalt are inappropriate.
c) that the Gestalt system can be helpful in aiding women to find their own power.*
d) self-in-relation is not always appropriate.

17. Gestalt therapists emphasize the importance of

a) past time orientation.
b) future time orientation.
c) present time orientation.*
d) integrating time in a complete holistic picture.

18. Logotherapy's time orientation places more on this dimension than other theories.

a) past time orientation.
b) future time orientation.*
c) present time orientation.
d) integrating time in a complete holistic picture.

19. According to the text, Gestalt's greatest influence on the field has been through

a) a set of powerful techniques.*
b) theoretical sophistication.
c) the life Perls himself.
d) a and b.
e) all of the above.

20. Perls and Gestalt therapy are most often associated with

a) cognitive-behavioral theory.

b) existential-humanistic theory.*
c) psychodynamic theory.
d) multicultural theory.

Essay Questions

1. Compare and contrast microskill and empathic dimensions as they are used in Rogerian, Gestalt, and logotherapy orientations.

2. What are the implications of (Gestalt, logotherapy) for gender and multicultural counseling and therapy? Provide both a criticism and a response so that they theories are made more culturally relevant.

3. Frankl is often termed one of the first cognitive theorists. How can this statement be justified?

4. Define the key logotherapy strategy of modification of attitudes. What implications does it have for treatment? How might it be used in multicultural counseling and therapy?

5. Develop an alcohol treatment program using aspects of cognitive-behavioral theory and logotherapy.

6. Logotherapy is a very verbal, often formal operational, set of techniques. How could these concepts be made more concrete in nature? How would you adapt these techniques so that clients can become more aware of themselves in a systemic, contextual world (dialectic/systemic operations)?

SUGGESTED SUPPLEMENTARY READING

Frankl, V. *Man's Search for Meaning.* New York: Pocket, 1959.

> Short, powerful, and moving, this book is one which can make a difference in your life and that of your clients. The authors consider this book one of the essential tools of any counselor or therapist.

Lukas, E. *Meaningful Living: A Logotherapy Book.* Berkeley, CA: The Institute of Logotherapy, 1984.

> Viktor Frankl's student and colleague presents the how of logotherapy with case examples and specific techniques to enable the enactment of Frankl's important philosophy.

Perls, F. *Gestalt Therapy Verbatim.* Moab, UT: Real People Press, 1969.

A series of typescripts by the master therapist with interesting commentary and theoretical insertions.

Perls, F. *In and Out of the Garbage Pail.* Moab, UT: Real People Press, 1969.

An autobiography of Perls complete with drawings and personal ramblings on a multitude of issues. Delightful to some, appalling to others.

Chapter 13

Toward an Integrated Counseling and Therapy

Overview

As I indicate in the introduction, I like to have students read this concluding chapter at the very beginning of the course and then read it again at the end. I do this because I want students to answer the ten questions about their own construction of counseling and psychotherapy process and I want them to think about this issue throughout the course. Similarly, I want them to think constantly about their own worldview. **No multiple choice or essay questions are presented.**

This chapter is basically a summation of the entire book and the summary chart presenting an overview of the four major forces can be helpful to students in mapping out the field.

The concepts of this chapter are few in number, but are all important:

> *The growth of eclecticism.* As I note in the introduction, I think the eclectic position is often a good one, but I have been influenced by George Kelly who in 1955 commented that as eclecticism becomes more integrated and systematic, it approaches a theory in its own right.
>
> The position of this book is greatly changed since the first edition where we advocated each person choosing his own theory. We now advocate for all theories and the importance of theoretical integration. We still recommend that students generate their own integration, but we are clearly urging them to consider seriously all the ideas of this book. Research and clinical experience suggests that they work.
>
> *The four major forces of counseling and psychotherapy* are presented in chart form.
>
> *The case management framework* is summarized briefly and related to network therapy.
>
> *Qualitative research issues* are summarized and an exhibit recommends that some form of research and evaluation be used with each interviewing case.
>
> *Students are encouraged to generate their own worldview and construction of counseling and psychotherapy.*

Class Procedures

1. Eclecticism, Single Theory, or Integrated Theory? At this point, I fear I am repeating myself to my students, but we go over the values of each theory and discuss the multicultural implications of them all. We spend a considerable time discussing "how can we do it all?" Students find the idea that all theories have value attractive, but realize that they can't be immediately effective in all. We talk about a lifetime of learning and growth in the field.

Each student is encouraged to generate her or his own integration and I refer frequently to pages 369 and 372 where they are asked to generate their own statements on the field. As much as time permits this late in the term, I like to hear from students in as much depth as possible. If I had a small seminar, I would like each to share their frame of reference with the entire class. As this isn't possible, the next best thing seems to be a paper.

2. Case Management and Network Therapy. I tend to summarize this material briefly and then ask them in small groups to work the ideas of case management. We discuss the pros and cons of case management. Many psychology and counseling trainees don't like the idea of case management while social workers and elementary counselors often recognize it as essential. What does seem clear is that one single intervention from one helper is seldom enough to produce change, particularly if you endorse the multicultural approach.

3. Qualitative research. The course emphasized the scientist-practitioner and the research presentation is an attempt to point out that all therapists and counselors can be scientist-practitioners. Accountability is coming of age in our field and individually-negotiated goals and qualitative research techniques such as those emphasized in the chapter may be part of our long-term salvation in this area.

My next hope is that qualitative research techniques such as the ones stressed here can be used in practicum courses.

Assignments

I ask students to complete the two important exercises in this chapter:

> Worldview exercise to codify their construction of how they see their purpose and values in counseling and therapy.
>
> Ten questions exercise to start the lifelong process of constructing one's own view of the field.

Section III

Portfolio of Competencies

Counseling and Therapy: A Multicultural Perspective contains a fairly large number of interviewing/counseling/clinical competencies which show students how to take theory into direct practice. We have found that students at first are a bit reluctant to engage in the practice exercises, but that as time goes by they realize the value of practice before they enter practicum. Both experienced interviewers and beginners enjoy presenting their work at the conclusion of a course.

There are more competencies presented than can be completed in one term. You can view the ones I select for my own courses in the sample syllabus. However, I have used all the suggested competencies and know that they are valuable. I would recommend you select the ones which are most relevant to your students and your situation. Then, suggest that students examine the competencies which are not completed and follow-up with them at a later point.

This Fourth Edition has an even stronger emphasis on competencies. The more we use these competencies, we find that students rate our classes more highly and as more valuable. We urge you to consider moving to this practical emphasis. Students seem to learn more about theory the more they start practice exercises.

Some of the competencies are self-understanding exercises which help build clinical/counseling competencies. I like to insert selected competencies in the syllabus, but I have sometimes simply duplicated the entire list of competencies and encourage students to select those which are to be completed.

In addition, feedback over the years tells me that many students save this book and the competencies and continue working on them during their professional careers.

The competencies associated with each chapter include. We have made a few comments on some competencies which we find particularly helpful.

Taking Theory into Practice: Specific Strategies for Mastery and Action in the Interview

Chapter 1: Introduction and Overview

1.1 The Community Genogram: Identifying Strengths
If we are to move toward a counseling and psychotherapy which is fully aware of context, this exercise is vital. The positive strengths and understanding which comes from the community genogram offer a highly

useful framework for a culture-centered therapy which does not stereotype clients, but rather helps find uniqueness and individuality.

Chapter 2: The Empathic Attitude: Individual, Family, and Culture

2.1 Acceptance as the Foundation of Empathy
We find this a particular useful exercises to use in the classroom.

2.2 The Positive Asset Search: Building Empathy on Strengths
Too much attention is paid to problems. I go back to Leona Tyler's powerful "minimal change therapy" where she showed me how important it is to work with clients from a positive frame of reference. Her lesson still has not been learned by our profession.

2.3 Identifying Yourself as a Multicultural Being
The multicultural cube is a useful way to help students realize that biculturality or multiculturality affects us all. Multiculturalism is for us all, not for a small minority group. We can all profit from seeing ourselves as multicultural beings.

2.4 Developing a Family Chart/Genogram
If students have completed both a community and family chart, they have the foundations for seeing people-in-context and useful assessment/teaching tools for the counseling and therapy interview.

Chapter 3: Conducting an Intentional Interview: Theory, Skills, Decisions, and Solutions

3.1 Using the Basic Listening Sequence to Draw Out a Client's Story
As you will note, we have placed microskills as a technology of constructivist and social-constructivist thought. We also use the microskills now to introduce narrative theory. If your students have a strong skill base, this practice exercise need only be reviewed briefly. If they are new to the skills approach, it is most useful.

3.2 Reframing Client Stories
As I write this, I find I am not setting up priorities. I recognize we can't do it all, but I like this one as well. Reframing seems to be replacing the word interpretation and is an increasingly useful skill to help clients see new frames of reference.

3.3 Decisional Counseling
An essential skill for vocational counseling and any decisional work.

3.4 Solution-Oriented Counseling and Therapy
New to this book, I have found that microskills and solutions work together rather nicely. This exercise is obviously only a beginning, but it is helpful in orienting students to an increasingly popular approach to helping.

Chapter 4: Developmental Counseling and Therapy: Integrating Alternative Perspectives

4.1 Assessing client meaning-making within four cognitive-developmental orientations. The exercise here can be done in class. I also like to show videotapes of the orientations and to have students start assessing meaning-making systems as part of their regular practice sessions.

4.2 Utilizing specific questions to facilitate client conversation and narratives within the four cognitive-developmental orientations. Another basic exercise which can enable more understanding and effectiveness as students move to other theories.

4.3 Examining one's family of origin and how we co-construct meaning, thoughts, behaviors, and relationships.
This is a powerful exercise and can generate more than a full class hour of discussion and evaluation.

4.4 Utilize specific questions to facilitate family conversation and narratives within the four cognitive-developmental orientations.
Shows how to use DCT with families.

4.5 Identifying your own personal style, present competencies, and counseling and therapeutic goals.
This is a brief, but important self-assessment exercise for students. It helps them look at where they are at, and suggests directions for the future.

Chapter 5: Multicultural Counseling and Therapy I: Metatheory Taking Theory into Practice.

5.1 Generating Culturally-Relevant Theories of Helping
To complete this competency could involve a full dissertation and it did for Uchenna Nwachuku. But, I have found that students can do this exercise in a brief form and understand that they can develop some of their own ways of looking at the interview. This is an empowerment exercise for many.

5.2 Naikan Therapy and Self-in-Relation
This is perhaps the most controversial of all the competencies. It is directly opposite to many Western notions of therapy. If presented with care, a beginning understanding of Naikan can be obtained. But more important is to help students realize that their discomfort with this approach may be similar to a Japanese person who encounters U.S. methods. The jarring effect of difference should be noted. See my syllabus for ideas on how to present this material to students for an exercise.

5.3 Developmental Mapping and Story Telling
Developmental theory can be used in the interview. This is a most useful set of experiences to help students think more developmentally.

5.4 Basic Consciousness-Raising
Another controversial exercise. You can get lots of class discussion around the merits of this one.

5.5 Using the Circle of Life for Decision Making
Sunny Hansen's comprehensive framework is a wonderful synthesis of the Minnesota model and feminist thinking. It is useful for both men and women.

Chapter 6: Multicultural Counseling and Therapy II: Metatheory Taking Theory into Practice.

6.1 Introductory Exercise in Feminist Therapy
Great fun to have men think about themselves from this perspective. As far as we can tell, this book remains the only one with a commitment to women's issues and women's theory.

6.2 Examining Oneself and Others as Multicultural Beings
A repeat of Chapter 3 exercise as a deeper level.

6.3 Basic Meditation
Vital CBT exercise which is really derived from multicultural theory.

6.4 Family Rules and Roles in Client Daily Life
Another useful exercise for individual growth and in the clinical or counseling interview.

6.5 Psychotherapy as Liberation
For understanding of the *how* of multicultural counseling, this exercise is a necessity. It builds on the community genogram, the family chart, DCT, and multicultural theory. It is a highly specific and useful system to help people debrief and think about their experience with oppression in new ways.

Chapter 7: Psychodynamic Counseling and Psychotherapy: Conception and Theory

7.1 Generating a Psychodynamic Developmentally-Oriented Treatment Plan
I find that conceptualizing treatment plans is where this theory shines. Students may not want to practice psychodynamically, but understanding complex developmental roots of difficulties can be most beneficial regardless of the direction one takes in terms of treatment.

Chapter 8: Psychodynamic Counseling and Psychotherapy: Applications for Practice

8.1 Focused Free Association
This is a basic exercise and with understanding it can be used with CBT and other forms of helping. It is an underemphasized strategy which does not have to be tied to psychodynamic practice.

8.2 Free Association Exercises and Techniques
As time permits, these are all useful.

8.3 Focused Free Association and Guided Imagery with Gender, Spiritual, and Cultural Symbols
Developed by DCT theory, this strategy is useful for building positive strengths.

8.4 Psychodynamic Interviewing
We encourage our students to actually try a dream analysis and they are surprised to find that "it works" and that it can be beneficial to clients.

Chapter 9: Cognitive-Behavioral Counseling and Therapy: Behavioral Foundations

All of the following impress me and our group as essential. CBT has a strong positive impact on our field and all these skills can be considered essential. At issue, of course, is how many can we select in one course?

9.1 Applied Behavioral Analysis
Too many, in my opinion, omit this exercise. It really can help students learn how to think about behavior. It is an excellent foundation for understanding CBT and other forms of theory.
9.2 Relaxation Training
9.3 Systematic Desensitization, Constructing an Anxiety Hierarchy
9.4 Social Skills Training
9.5 Assertiveness Training
9.6 Relapse Prevention
9.7 Stress Management Programs

Chapter 10: Cognitive-Behavioral Counseling and Therapy: Cognitive and Integrative Approaches

Again, all of the following seem essential. My experience is gradually moving me more to Glasser and Reality Therapy. This surprises me, but he has such a good grasp of the environment. This does not obviate the useful thinking of Ellis and the wonderful automatic thoughts exercise. For treatment planning, Lazarus is most helpful.

10.1 Rational Emotive Behavior Therapy Self-Help Form
10.2 Automatic thoughts Within Gender and Multicultural Context

10.3 Reality Therapy Including Contextual and Multicultural Cognitive Issues
10.4 Exploring the BASIC ID

Chapter 10: The Existential-Humanistic Tradition: Existential-Humanistic Theory and Person-Centered Theory and Practice

11.1 Conducting a "Non-Directive Interview"
As you will note from my syllabus, I try to integrate this material with the microskills concepts.

11.2 Integrating Existential/Humanistic and Multicultural Issues in the Interview
Vontress offers us a new challenge. We will be interested in your feedback about our new emphasis on spirituality.

Chapter 12: The Existential-Humanistic Tradition: logotherapy and Experiential Gestalt Therapy

12.1 Finding New Meanings in the Interview Via Logotherapy
The five-stage structure is useful as a way to start thinking about mean-making.

12.2 The Gestalt Empty Chair Technique and Resolving Unfinished Business
Student always enjoy Perls' powerful technique. I still use his word and admire his thinking immensely.

Chapter 13: Toward an Integrated Counseling and Psychotherapy

13.1 Defining Your Counseling and Therapy Worldview
An important conclusion to a course such as this is encouraging students to generate their own integration of all this material. This exercise and the following are useful as final papers.

13.2 Ten Questions to Ask Yourself about Your Own Construction of the Counseling and Psychotherapy Process
This is also a good place for students to review the competencies they have mastered.

Section IV

Example Syllabus

The following syllabus was designed for a combination graduate and undergraduate course. As such, it gives more attention to beginning skills and concepts. With more advanced students, we recommend more time and attention to more complex competencies and perhaps more attention to cognitive-behavioral theory and practice. In addition, there is more time for the several MCT exercises. With a 15 week course, we recommend two weeks on the DCT chapter. The skills generated there will be most useful in accomplishing the objectives later in the book.

The practice competencies are really the main contribution of this text, in our opinion. Again and again, we find that students develop a cognitive understanding of theory best by actually engaging in concrete practice. Select those practice exercises that best meet the needs of your students.

Theory and Practice of Interviewing and Counseling
Fall 1996

> The provision of professional services to persons of culturally different backgrounds by persons not competent in understanding and providing professional services to such group shall be considered unethical: . . . it shall be equally unethical to deny such persons professional services because the present staff is inadequately prepared; . . . it shall be the obligation of all service agencies to employ competent persons or to provide continuing education for the present staff to meet the service needs of the culturally diverse population it serves. (Korman, 1973, p. 105)
>
> These *General Guidelines* have been developed with the understanding that . . . services must be planned and implemented so that they are sensitive to factors related to life in a pluralistic society such as age, gender, affectional orientation, cultural, and ethnicity. (American Psychological Association, *Guidelines for Providers of Psychological Services,* 1987. p. 1)

Introduction

We face a time in counseling and therapy where the history of cultural and professional racism and oppression needs to be reviewed. Psychology and counseling have in many ways operated without awareness of multicultural context and there is much change which needs to occur. Let us participate in a reconceptualized profession of helping.

Counseling and therapy are also moving rapidly toward new conceptions of theory and treatment. This course is designed to provide you with specific alternatives for treatment of a variety of clients. The field is currently moving rapidly toward what is termed "differential treatment." In the past we have focused on "What is the best theory of counseling and therapy?" and counselors and therapist trainees have been encouraged to make their own integration.

Developing one's own integration of counseling and therapy theory will remain important in the future, but we are also finding that certain types of treatment are likely to be more effective than others with some clients. As such we have a responsibility to learn treatments and theories which are not always comfortable for us. We may not practice these methods, but we need to know enough about them to make intelligent referrals.

In this course, we believe in alternative perspectives on the truth. We encourage you to generate your own construction of the counseling and psychotherapy process. At the same time, we ask you to respect and seek to understand the constructions and worldviews of people different from you.

Course Objectives

If this course is successful you may be able to:

1. *Describe and understand the major concepts of foundational theories of helping.* This includes the empathic dimensions, the microskills and decisional counseling, and developmental counseling and therapy. As part of this process you will be introduced to solution-oriented counseling and therapy.

2. *Describe and understand the four major forces of counseling and psychotherapy:* First force, psychodynamic theory, second force cognitive-behavioral theory, third force existential-humanistic theory, and fourth force multicultural counseling and therapy.

3. *Describe and understand some basics of family theory.* This course states that the individual develops in a family in a cultural context. An understanding of all three dimensions are vital for effective individual, family, or group counseling and therapy.

4. *Generate a portfolio of interviewing competencies.* This course seeks to prepare you to engage in some of the basics of interviewing in the belief that it is critical to take theory directly into practice. Instructions for this portfolio are presented both in this syllabus and the attached statement.

5. *Develop an ethically and multiculturally aware understanding of the field.* Ethics, which includes multicultural and gender

sensitivity, must undergird both course presentations, your practice exercises, and later your own professional work.

Course Requirements

1. Portfolio of Competencies. Each week during the course, you will be given an assignment which typically focuses on some activity emphasizing personal understanding of the material and/or interviewing practice itself. These are all oriented toward more effective interviewing, counseling, and therapy practice. These will be viewed weekly and are to be presented again at the conclusion of the term in portfolio form with a self-evaluation of your work.

2. Midterm examination. A multiple-choice and essay examination will be presented at midterm.

3. Final paper. This paper may be of two types: 1) it may be an in-depth theoretical summary of your work in this course as outlined in the final chapter of the text; or 2) it may be a transcript of an interview in which you analyze your work form a variety of perspectives. Instructions for the transcript are attached to this syllabus.

Textbooks for this Course

Ivey, A., Ivey, M., and Simek-Morgan, L. (1997) *Counseling and Psychotherapy From a Multicultural Perspective.* (4th Ed.) Boston: Allyn & Bacon.

Frankl, V. *Man's Search for Meaning.* (1959) New York: Pocket.

Ivey, A., Gluckstern, N., and Ivey, M. (1992) *Basic Attending Skills.* North Amherst, Ma: Microtraining.

WEEKLY READINGS AND ASSIGNMENTS

Try to complete readings before each class. Thus, the first week, you do have three chapters to read so that you are ready for the second week.

Assignments are always due the following week. One grade is dropped for each late week unless prior arrangements are made. Please use word processor or typewriter for all homework and papers.

Week 1 Introduction

Reading: C& P: Chapters 1 and 13. Chapter 13 will help you see where the course is going and may be referred to from time to time as you develop your own personal integration of the material. Handout on professional ethics.

Portfolio of Competencies: All assignments due the following week.

1. Worldview preliminary statement. Develop a preliminary one-page statement on your own worldview–**see page 369, Exhibit 14.1 for ideas.** Two pages is fine for a start. This can be developed as the term permits, but it is important to start on this process early so that you can relate various theories of counseling and psychotherapy to your own evolving worldview. During the term, look at your statement and revise it for your final portfolio.

2. Community Genogram. Practice Exercise 1.1 (page 11) presents instructors for the first counseling/clinical competency of this course. Please interview a volunteer client or classmate and generate with them a community genogram. Report on your experience in from two to three pages.

Week 2 The Empathic Conditions: Derived from Carl Rogers

Reading: C & P Chapter 2. You may want to read Chapter 11 material on Rogers in advance as his ideas are particularly important in the early phases of this course.

Portfolio of Competencies: All assignments due the following week.

3. Genogram and cultural influences on your development. Our ideas about the world are most often constructed in reaction to or in relationship to our families of origin. Construct a genogram of three generations of your family using the guidelines on pages 43. Then complete the exercise in cultural awareness, Exhibit 2.3 page 39. How does your family background and influence relate to your own personal images of yourself as a cultural being.

Additional graduate student competency, Using the Genogram in the Interview. With a volunteer client, develop a genogram. This can be a very helpful assessment device in helping you and the client understand developmental history.

Week 3 Microskills: Listening Skills Derived from Carl Rogers

Reading: C & P, Chapter 3, *Basic Attending Skills,* Entire book. Give special attention to attending behavior and the basic listening sequence. Also handout on classification of listening skills.

Portfolio of Competencies:

4. Attending behavior and observation skills: Observe other people in interpersonal interaction this coming week. Using attending behavior concepts as a guideline, what do you observe about these personal contacts? How do you find people listening? What nonverbal observations do you note? During the week, at least once, deliberately engage in non-attending behavior, note the other person's response, then reengage with good attending skills. What do you observe? Write down your observations in two pages.

Additional graduate student competency. An important role of the professional helper is teaching skills of interviewing to paraprofessionals, community volunteers, teachers, parents, or other groups. Use the microskills framework to teach helping skills to a small group of four or more and report back on your results.

5. Focusing. Conduct a ten-minute or more role-played interview with a volunteer client and audiotape or videotape the session. Using primarily listening skills, seek to focus one-third of the time on the individual, one-third on family, and one-third on cultural/contextual issues. Suggested topics for the interview are:

1) vocational decision (the individual makes a choice, but the family certainly influences that choice. Work and how it is done is deeply affected by the cultural context),
2) men's or women's issues (how the individual feels about the issues, how the family feels, and how cultural prescriptions set up the way we see and do things). Present 3-5 pages in which you provide transcript examples of each focus and your personal analysis of what happened.

Week 4 Microskills: Influencing Skills and Strategies, Focusing and Multicultural Issues

Reading: C & P, Chapter 3 with special attention to decisional counseling and the five-stages of the interview and solution-oriented approaches.
Start reading Frankl's *Man's Search for Meaning.*

Portfolio of Competencies:

6. Complete on of the following or do both for extra credit. Practice Exercise 3.3 (page 81) on Decisional Counseling and the five stages of the interview and/or Practice Exercise 3.4 (page 83) on solution-oriented counseling and therapy.

Week 5 Developmental Counseling and Therapy

Reading: C & P, Chapter 4, pages 89-114—DCT theory and its applications to the individual)

Portfolio of Competencies:

7. Developmental Strategies Questioning Sequence. Complete Exhibit 4.2, page 107, with a volunteer client and write a report on what occurred. Graduate students will be expected to provide written examples for the interview which indicate that they indeed were able to help their clients take all four perspectives on the single issue. *Note: the sensorimotor questions can be very powerful. Please use these with ethics and care as we have talked about them in class.*

8. Identifying your own personal style, present competencies, and goals. Complete Practice Exercise 4.5, page 126. This will help you evaluate your present understanding of the field and help establish some goals for the future.

Week 6 The Existential-Humanistic Tradition: Carl Rogers and Victor Frankl

Reading: *C & P,* Chapters 11 and 12

Portfolio of Competencies:

9. An Exercise in Person-Centered Counseling. Complete the Exercise in Exhibit **11.2, pages 300-301** and write a two-three page report on its effectiveness. Make a very serious effort not to use questions any more than absolutely necessary.

or

9a. An Exercise in Logotherapy. **Complete Exhibit 12.1 on pages 319-320.**

Week 7 Multicultural Counseling and Therapy

Reading: *C & P,* Chapter 5

Portfolio of Competencies:

10. Naikan therapy. This exercise will likely be jarring to you. It is designed to introduce you to a very different way of thinking about the helping field. Either try this exercise on yourself (Practice Exercise 5.2, page 150) or find a volunteer client who is willing to take a different look at her or himself than is usually expected as we think about counseling and therapy.

11. Exercise in developmental mapping and storytelling. Practice Exercise 5.3 (page 156) will be helpful in generating an understanding of how developmental issues over the life span can be integrated into counseling.

12. Your own cultural identity. Practice Exercise 5.6 asks you to examine yourself and your relationship to cultural identity theory.

Additional graduate student competency. Cultural Values and Culturally Relevant Theories of Helping. Practice Exercise 5.1 on page 143 talks about how to develop new and perhaps more culturally-relevant theory (any multicultural group including ethnicity/race, religion, age, gender, affectional orientation, etc.). Take a group or culture of interest to you and generate a brief outline of a theory using the guidelines suggested there. One way to present this is in chart form where you contrast one culture with another—for example traditional European-American culture as whole with Polish-American, Northern African-Americans contrasted with Southern African-Americans, gays contrasted with straights, etc. *Be sure not to stereotype a group in this process.*

Week 8: Multicultural Counseling and Therapy II.

Reading: Chapter 6

Portfolio of Competencies:

12. Feminist theory and practice. Complete Practice Exercise 6.1 (page 177). Gender analysis is critical to this process, whether working with men or women.

13, Psychotherapy as liberation. Practice Exercise 6.5 is particularly important (page 199). This exercise summarizes the first eight chapters of this book in an integrated fashion.

Extra credit competency, network therapy. Generate a network treatment plan for a specific problem or difficulty of interest to you(for example, borderline personality style, delinquency, alcohol or substance abuse, bulimia, etc.).

Week 9 Midterm Examination and Plan Ahead for Final Papers

Reading: Reread, *C & P.*, Chapter 13.

Also pay special attention to final paper instructions. Your final paper in this course may be of two types, but each type should include the information on your own worldview.

What is your Counseling and Therapy Worldview. Include with your interview presentation, the information of Exhibit 14.1, page 369 above or include this same information with your final paper answering the ten questions on page 372.
Interview presentation and analysis. Conduct an interview of 30 minutes or more. Using the model in the handout for transcript analysis, transcribe, present, and analyze your work. *Attached to this syllabus is information on how to set this task and present it.*

***What is Your Construction of the Counseling and Psychotherapy Process?* Answer the ten questions on pages 372-373, Exhibit 14.3**

Week 10 Psychodynamic Theory and Practice

Reading: C & P Chapter 7

Portfolio of Competencies:

14. Generating a Psychodynamically-Oriented Treatment Plan. Practice Exercise 7.1 (page 237) will enable you to integrate the theoretical ideas of this chapter in a very practical way. Select a personality style/disorder of interest to you and work your way through this useful exercise. You may be surprised to find how able you are in understanding and conceptualizing these issues.

Week 11 Psychodynamic Counseling and Therapy II

Reading: C & P Chapter 8. This chapter shows how to integrate theory and practice through direct application of psychodynamic theory.

12. Free association. Write up your own experience of the free association exercise Practice Exercise 8.1 on page 244.

or

12a. Focused Free Association and Guided Imagery Using Gender, Religious, and Cultural Symbols. Complete Practice Exercise 8.3 on page 247.

Extra credit competencies, Free Association Exercises and Techniques. Exhibit 8.2 (page 244) contains an array of special exercises related to the psychodynamic orientation.

Graduate Students Only: An Exercise in Psychodynamic Interviewing. Exhibit 8.4 (page 250) presents the specifics of a psychodynamically-oriented session using the five-stage interview model.

Week 12 Cognitive-Behavioral Therapy, Part I (Focus on Stress Management)

Reading: *C & P,* Chapter 9

Portfolio of Competencies:

13 and 14. Select two of the following and write a report on your experience. In each of the following, note the importance of

Relaxation training. Take a volunteer client through one of the two relaxation exercises on page 288, Practice Exercise 9.2. Or make an audiotape adapting the relaxation suggestions to your own style, listen to it yourself and modify as necessary, then write a report on your experience.

Construct in anxiety hierarchy. Using the model on pages 293-294, Practice Exercise 9.3 construct an anxiety hierarchy on examination anxiety or some other issues with a volunteer client. *Graduate students only, systematic desensitization.* Take a volunteer client through systematic desensitization.

Teaching attending skills. Using the microskills, teach a client effective attending behavior and the use of questions. See page 297, Practice Exercise 9.4. These two social skills can be very helpful to a number of clients, particularly those who are depressed, lack social skills, may be shy (or avoidant), or who may be too self-centered to listen to others.

Assertiveness training. Take a volunteer through the Assertiveness Training Exercises in Practice Exercise 9.4., pages 298-299. Discuss the assertiveness issue from a multicultural perspective with your client and ensure that the assertiveness you teach is culturally and individually appropriate for your client.

Applied Behavioral Analysis. Complete the Exercises in Applied Behavioral Analysis, Practice Exercise 9.1, pages 282-284. No exercise can be more helpful than this in learning how to facilitate concreteness and clarity of expression in clients, regardless of your ultimate theoretical orientation.

Stress management. Write a stress management program for a specific population and, if possible, teach the program and supply feedback from your participants. See Practice Exercise 9.7, page 305.

Week 13 Cognitive-Behavioral Counseling and Therapy: Cognitive Approaches

Reading: *C & P,* Chapter 10

Portfolio of Competencies:

15. and 16. Select two of the following, according to your interests and preferences:

A-B-C Analysis. Complete Practice Exercise 10.1, the Rational-Emotive Therapy Self-Help Form, page 320 with a volunteer client.

12-Step Alcohol program. Visit an AA, ACOA, or other alcohol treatment group. Demonstrate your awareness of 12-step programs.

Using alcohol/substance abuse idea as in the individual interview. Generate a plan to integrate alcohol and substance abuse treatment in your own individual therapy and counseling.

Automatic thoughts. Help a volunteer client through Beck's automatic thoughts daily record, Practice Exercise 10.2, pages 331-332. Follow-up and discuss with the client, her or his discoveries.

Exercise in Reality Therapy. Take a client through the interview using Practice Exercise 10.3, page 336 as your model.

The Basic Id. Practice Exercise 10.4, page 344 will give you a basic understanding of Lazarus' organizing frame.

Week 14 Family Counseling and Therapy

Reading: Read or reread C & P pages 40ff, 67, 68, 69, 114ff, 186ff, 224ff, 261-262, 330, 411-412

Portfolio of competencies:

17. Family rules in individual counseling. Complete Practice Exercise 4.3, page 115-116.

18. SCDT Questioning Sequence. Practice exercise 4.4 (page 120) will provide an integrative practice session for you in which you will demonstrate your ability to use most of the skills and concepts of this book in a family session.

19. Review the book from a family perspective. The text argues that individual work is incomplete without a family perspective. What are your current thoughts on this issue? How will you integrate family ideas into your own approach to counseling and therapy?

Final Instructions for Course

To complete this course, you need to turn in the following:

1. Portfolio of Competencies. Please pass in again all of the competencies you have completed to date. If you have added any new material, revised any competency, please indicate it clearly.

Organize your portfolio as follows:

1. An overview of your evaluation of learnings from the portfolio. List your strengths and areas where you feel you need further development in these skills and strategies.

2. Competencies completed. Please place a Scotch tape tab on new or revised material so that we can give you feedback more easily.

2. One of the following (see Midterm Examination for more specifics)

1. Transcript of interview with complete analysis, including detailed statement on worldview.

2. Answers to ten questions on page 418, Practice Exercise 13.2, including detailed statement on worldview.

COURSE REQUIREMENTS

1. Attendance. As this course will be highly experiential with practice exercises and only meets once a week, attendance at all sessions is critical. One unexcused cut will be allowed. A written request for more than one cut will be required in advance.

2. Competencies The weekly assignments are extremely important to help the instructors keep in touch with you and your progress. The lowest two marks on competencies or two missing assignments) will be dropped when computing your final mark. Or you are free to redo the competency if you wish.

3. Papers. Please type or use a word processor for all papers Leave us room in the margins for comments. Please include cassettes of your interviews with your major papers.

4. Examinations. There will be a midterm. The exam will be some combination of short answer, essay and objective questions.

5. Weighting: Class participation and attendance: 10%
Portfolio of Competencies: 40%
Paper or transcript: 40%
Midterm: 10%

6. Grading criteria:

A: Excellent performance on all of above

A/B: Excellent performance on 75% of above

B: Excellent or good performance on 50% of above and satisfactory on remainder

B/C: Excellent or good performance on 25% of above and satisfactory on remainder

C: Satisfactory performance on all of above

Lower than C: Less than satisfactory

7. Academic difficulties. In a large University, a student can sometimes find him or herself overwhelmed by classes or other issues. We are anxious to be of assistance. If you find yourself having difficulty in this course, please contact us immediately. Usually, we can be of assistance.

8. Late paper policy. Late assignments will receive one grade cut per week unless written agreement is made ahead of time. If you are going to a wedding or something similar, just let us know ahead of time in writing. We really want to be flexible and supportive.

9. Incompletes. No incompletes will be offered in this course except for medical causes or\personal emergency. The University now requires us to have a written contract for any incomplete. As such, we cannot turn in an incomplete grade without a written contract for completion which specifies for you and for us what must be done. Without this contract, we will have to turn in an **F** even if your work is satisfactory. (The F, of course, could be changed later through negotiation with the professor - but the hassles of grade changes at U. Mass. are many. It will be easier to finish the course or to write the specific contract for completion.

CONFIDENTIALITY AND ETHICS INFORMATION

In this course, you are entering an experience which involves a fair amount of role-playing and practice interviewing. Naturally, in the course of discussion, it is possible for a student colleague to say something personally important and confidential. It is your duty to maintain confidentiality and trust. These same principles hold when talking to your clients. Papers which do not disguise the nature of the individual with whom you are talking will not be accepted. Papers which do not indicate that you have the permission of the client to turn in this paper, even though the identity is disguised, will not be accepted.

At the same time keep in mind the legal limits of confidentiality. You have no legal right to maintain confidence if you were questioned by an attorney in court. Study the ethics code, particularly paying attention to issues of confidentiality and client's rights.

When audio or video taping a session with a role-playing or real client, be sure you have permission on tape for that interview to proceed. If your client wishes, stop the tape at any time. When you present a typescript, be sure that the identity of your client is disguised and that you have indicated in your casenotes or report that you have permission to use the material.

FOR YOUR OWN CONSIDERATION IN YOUR OWN ROLE PLAYS AS CLIENT: You have the right and personal responsibility to only share of yourself what you want to talk about. All experiential exercises in this course are optional and you may stop participating in any experiential exercise you wish at any time without penalty. At the same time, if you find yourself not wishing to engage in the exercises, you may prefer to drop the course. This course, by its very nature, is experientially oriented.

THIS IS A PROFESSIONAL AND PREPROFESSIONAL COURSE. As such, we are working with practical material. We seek to regard you as developing professionals. If you prefer primarily to "think about theory", this is not the course to take.

Section V

FINAL EXAM: HOW CAN WE USE THEORY IN PRACTICE?

The following examination questions are obviously more than can be covered in a two-hour final. Sometimes questions of this type make up a take-home examination. The exam is oriented to integration of the text.

Please write you name on the examination (one point)

Part I. Transcript analysis of skills (24 points)

PLEASE READ THE TYPESCRIPT - THEN CLASSIFY EACH OF LIZ'S NUMBERED MICROSKILL LEADS (2 points each for a total of 24 points)
LIZ IS THE COUNSELOR (SHE IS PUERTO RICAN, MIDDLE-CLASS AND ACTIVELY PRACTICING CATHOLIC) AND JILL IS THE CLIENT. JILL IS A SENIOR IN COLLEGE AND IS A WHITE, MIDDLE CLASS LIBERAL PROTESTANT.

O? = open question, C? = closed question, E = Encourage, P = paraphrase, RF = reflection of feeling, S= summarization. IF THE LEAD INCLUDES A CONFRONTATION OF DISCREPANCY, PLEASE INDICATE THAT AS WELL WITH A C.

Recall that you can classify a lead with more than one category. Space is provided below each counselor statement for you to justify or explain your classification if you wish, but this is not necessary.

__________ **1) Liz: Before we begin, do I have your permission to tape this?**

1) Jill: Yes, that's fine.

__________ **2) Liz: What would you like to talk about in our time together?**

2) Jill: Well, I got some news a week ago that I want to talk to you about.

__________ **3) Liz: Could you tell me about this news?**

3) Jill: Well, its kind of hard. I found out a week ago that I'm pregnant. I only have another two weeks to decide if I'm going to have an abortion or not because I found out so late so I don't know what to do.

________4) **Liz: Would it be helpful if we looked at some of your feelings about this, some of your positive feelings and some of your negative feelings?**

4) Jill: My positive feelings are that it would be really neat in some ways to have the baby. This is my last year in college and I don't really feel that excited about it right now. I really wouldn't mind just sort of being with the baby instead. I love children. I've always wanted to have a baby and I don't like the idea of an abortion at all. So that's my feeling about going ahead.

________5) **Liz: As you talk about having the baby, you seem anxious and I hear a sadness in your voice.**

5) Jill: Well, there would be some hard things, like I don't have any income now and the father is back home in Puerto Rico. He was in school here for a year and now he's gone and he doesn't even know. I don't know when I'm going to see him again...we talked about next summer but it's going to be a long time.

________6) **Liz: M-hmm.**

6) Jill: So I would sort of be bringing the baby up by myself and I really don't have a source of income. I mean I could get a job somewhere like restaurant work, but that's sort of demeaning and it would be hard working those long hours with a baby and everything.

________7) **Liz: Yeah, that would be hard work. Let me see if I've got this straight. I'm hearing a couple of different things. One is that you are pregnant and that you are carrying a child which does feel good. Its good to have that life within you. The other is that you are in a situation in which some of the support that can really help when you are pregnant isn't there. The father is in Puerto Rico and he doesn't know you are pregnant. Your income isn't what you would like it to be right now.**

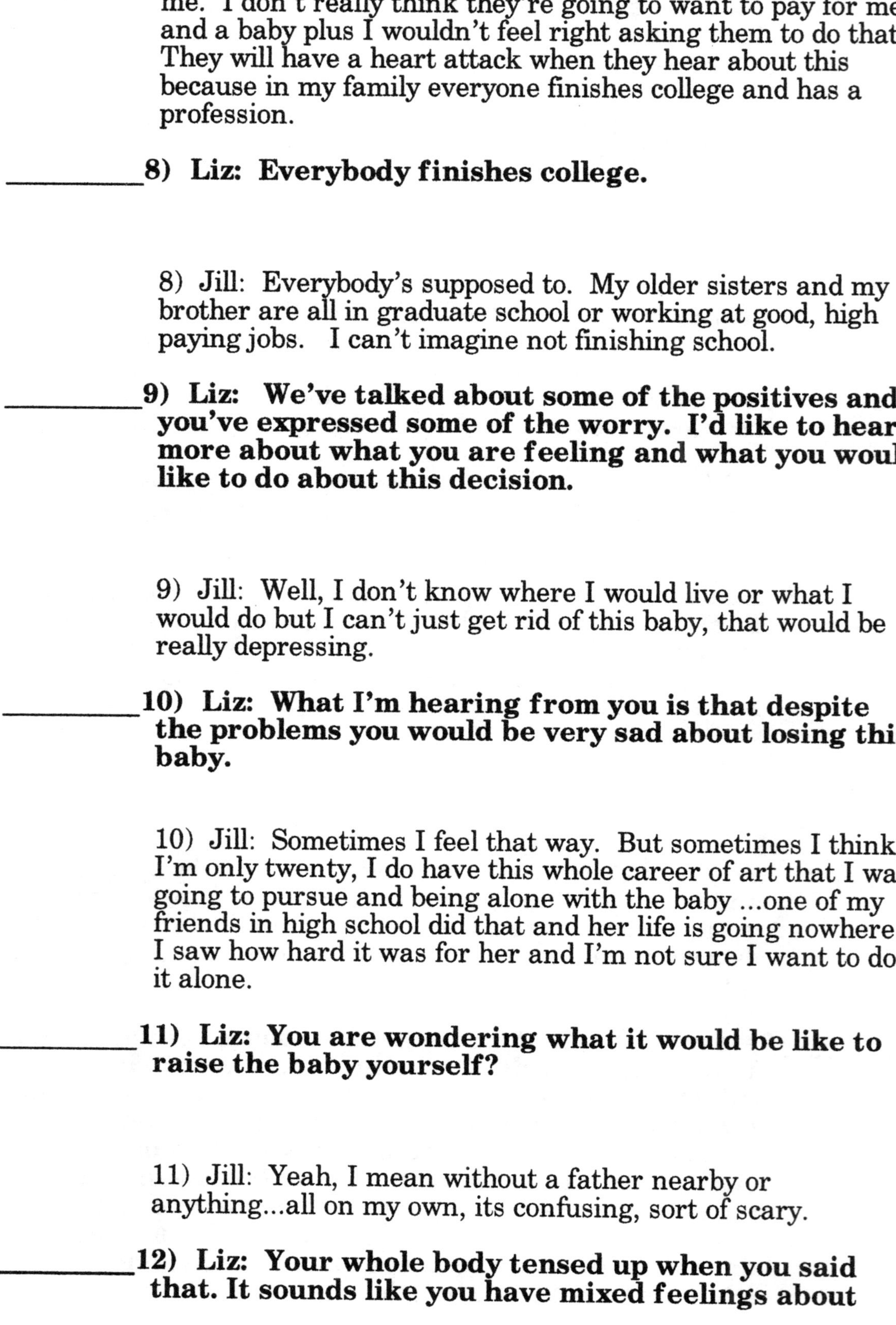

7) Jill: I'm going to school and my parents are supporting me. I don't really think they're going to want to pay for me and a baby plus I wouldn't feel right asking them to do that. They will have a heart attack when they hear about this because in my family everyone finishes college and has a profession.

__________**8) Liz: Everybody finishes college.**

8) Jill: Everybody's supposed to. My older sisters and my brother are all in graduate school or working at good, high paying jobs. I can't imagine not finishing school.

__________**9) Liz: We've talked about some of the positives and you've expressed some of the worry. I'd like to hear more about what you are feeling and what you would like to do about this decision.**

9) Jill: Well, I don't know where I would live or what I would do but I can't just get rid of this baby, that would be really depressing.

__________**10) Liz: What I'm hearing from you is that despite the problems you would be very sad about losing this baby.**

10) Jill: Sometimes I feel that way. But sometimes I think, I'm only twenty, I do have this whole career of art that I was going to pursue and being alone with the baby ...one of my friends in high school did that and her life is going nowhere. I saw how hard it was for her and I'm not sure I want to do it alone.

__________**11) Liz: You are wondering what it would be like to raise the baby yourself?**

11) Jill: Yeah, I mean without a father nearby or anything...all on my own, its confusing, sort of scary.

__________**12) Liz: Your whole body tensed up when you said that. It sounds like you have mixed feelings about**

this pregnancy. You feel happy and excited but also scared. Does that sound accurate?

Part II: Cognitive/Emotional Developmental Level (20 points)

1. What is Jill's (the client) predominant cognitive/emotional-developmental level? Justify your response. (10 points)

2. How could you use developmental skills to facilitate the client to talk and experience more at the sensori-motor level? (5 points)

3. How could you use developmental skills to facilitate the client to talk more at the dialectic-systemic level? (5 points)

Part III: Multicultural Issues (45) Points)

1. PLEASE WRITE AN ESSAY EXPLORING HOW THE CLIENT'S FAMILY AND CULTURAL CONTEXT AND HER GENDER MIGHT AFFECT HER SITUATION. YOU SHOULD ALSO CONSIDER HOW THE MAN'S CULTURAL BACKGROUND RELATES TO THIS CASE. (25 POINTS)

2. ASSUME THAT THE CLIENT IS AT A NAIVE LEVEL OF CONSCIOUSNESS ON WOMAN'S IDENTITY THEORY. HOW, SPECIFICALLY, COULD YOU HELP HER BECOME MORE GENDER CONSCIOUS USING FREIRE'S CONCEPTS OF *Conscientizacào* ? WHAT ETHICAL ISSUES OCCUR TO YOU AS YOU MIGHT DELIBERATELY WORK WITH A CLIENT TO CHANGE LEVEL OF CULTURAL IDENTITY? (20 points)

Part IV INTEGRATING FOUNDATIONAL AND HISTORICAL TREATMENTS WITH THE CLIENT (100 points)

Select five of the following for your response. (20 points each) Include multicultural/gender issues in your response to each theory,

1. Jill, the client, clearly has a decision to make. What techniques of decisional counseling might be helpful in this process?

2. Let us assume that Jill's indecision relates to some trauma experienced in her own family of origin. How might you use techniques of free association and regression to recover this experience? What are some professional and ethical issues in this process?

3. Assume that Jill does well with you in the first interview, but comes to the second very hostile and angry. You feel very defensive as the relationship had seemed fine in the first session—in fact you felt especially close to her and thought about her several times during the

week. You notice some small cuts on Jill's wrist. The interview is very intense and challenging and you felt exhausted afterwards. What is a possible developmental personality style that Jill might be manifesting? Given the style (or styles) you identify, what are some hypotheses you can make about this client as you plan for the next session?

4. Assume that Jill does well with you in the first session and continues to do well (specifically, none of the conditions of 2. and 3. above apply). However, assume that Jill is Puerto Rican herself and a Catholic. How might you adapt Rogerian person-centered counseling utilizing the concepts of self-in-relation of Jean Baker Miller to help her make an intelligent decision? What would be the nature of the relationship you would seek to establish with her?

5. Assume that Jill decides to meet with her manfriend, but feels unsure of what to say or do when they get together. How might you conduct an assertiveness practice session to help her?

6. Assume that while working with Jill, you discover that she suffers from a fear of heights. Construct an anxiety hierarchy and plan a systematic densensitization program for her.

7. Develop an individualized stress management program for Jill.

8. How could the concepts of cognitive approaches to CBT be useful to this client? Select the ideas of either Beck, Ellis, or Glasser for your response.

9. Abortion is an issue which involves meaning-making and values. Assume Jill has an abortion and then has difficulty dealing with this decision. What aspects of Frankl's logotherapy might be useful in helping Jill work with these issues? How would you use ideas of spirituality around this controversial issue?

10. Assume you decide that family therapy is to be your approach with this client. Outline some of the key issues you would explore and how you would use family theory to help this client.

Part V. Network Therapy (30 Points)

Assume Jill decides to carry the baby to term as a single parent. But, you find that she is very confused and lonely. She has a history of drinking and early in the pregnancy, she returns to this pattern. Assume she has a relatively supportive family. Develop a network treatment plan to help her work through and live with her issues.

STUDY GUIDE FOR FINAL EXAMINATION

There are 220 points in this examination. If you have any writing problems (e.g. dyslexia), please let us know. If you find writing in English causes you difficulty, we can arrange for extra time. The examination is designed as a learning activity and to help you organize the basics of the course.

1. One point- your name and section.

Part 1. 24 points. A brief counselor-client interaction will be presented and you will be asked to classify interviewing leads. One or more leads also contain a confrontation in which discrepancies in the client are confronted. Please note these. For preparation, practice classification of helping leads.

Part 2. 20 points. You will be asked to identify the predominant cognitive-developmental level of the client and suggest specific ways to help the client discuss issues at varying cognitive-developmental levels.

Part 3. 45 points. You will be asked to write an essay discussing the multicultural implications of the case. You will find an understanding of cultural identity theory and feminist theory helpful. Pay some attention as to how these issues can be used in the practical interviewing situation. Freire's concepts and Psychotherapy as Liberation will be especially helpful here. Know how to use and apply them with clients.

Part 4. 100 points. You will be asked to apply techniques from specific theories to the client in the transcript. Each of the theoretical chapters includes a number of practical applications of the theory. You need to be versed in those concepts and techniques and how you might apply them to a client. Be familiar with the major approaches and techniques of decisional counseling, psychodynamic counseling (including developmental personality style issues), person-centered, cognitive-behavioral and logotherapy. Be able to apply cultural/gender issues with these treatment techniques and theories.

Part 5. 30 points. Be able to develop a network treatment plan. DCT's framework, that of Carolyn Attneave's network therapy, Lazarus' BASIC-ID, and MCT will be useful in this regard.

Scoring Suggestions

1. 1 point for name

Part I. Typescript

1) closed question
2) open question
3) open question
4) open question
5) reflection of feelings (OK to add paraphrase, but must have RF)
6) encourage
7) summarization (also contains confrontation of discrepancies)
8) encourage
9) several possible here - paraphrase and reflection of feeling, for 2 points or summarization for 2.
10) paraphrase and reflection of feeling includes confrontation - need at least two of these to score 2
11) paraphrase
12) confrontation, reflection of feeling, summarization should contain at least two of the above

Also use your judgment and give one point when what they suggest makes some sense and the students provide a reasonable justification for a different response in the space provided.

Part II. Cognitive/Emotional Developmental Level

1. Five points for correct identification as formal. Example formal statements should be included as justification. As the client does present at several levels, allow partial credit if the justification is done correctly.

2. Questions focused on immediate here and now experience, imagining are the usual responses here ("What are you seeing, hearing, feeling?" or imagery exercises). Other sensorimotor techniques receive partial credit.

3) Culture and gender issues with special attention to family would be discussed at the dialectic/systemic level. Questions oriented to values and where those values come from would also be important. Examination of her role as a woman in society.

Part III. Multicultural Issues

Question 1.

1. Some intelligent discussion of the issue as a woman's issue
2. Some awareness of how being a liberal Protestant and *probably* supportive of choice relates to the issue.
3. Some awareness of the culture conflict and values about abortion between likely Roman Catholic Mexico and the liberal Protestant

culture. Also, it would be helpful if the roles of men and women in the two cultures is discussed.
4. Comment on any stereotyping - difficult... some Catholics favor choice, some Protestants are anti-abortion, etc. The word "some" helps qualify stereotyping. Five off for stereotyping.
5. The issue of family impact on the situation needs to be discussed.
6. Some discussion of feminist therapy would be helpful.
7. Social class issues are important - "I must finish college." the desire for achievement is particularly important.

Question 2.
1. The potential difficulty of the counselor's own Catholicism affecting the issue. Need some intelligent discussion of this issue. The counselor should not impose, but may gently express her own opinion. If the counselor feels too strongly, she may need to refer. The whole issue of spirituality should be considered.
2. The possibility of the counselor seeking support from the father should be considered. The client may need help and support here.
3. There should be some discussion of how the graduate student would act and how he or she would advise and support the counselor in the case. This is essential. Look for an intelligent responsible response.
4. For the cultural identity theory portion of this question, the student should work from Psychotherapy as Liberation. Thus, focusing on images, naming the problem, and other concepts referred to in the chapter on MCT are important.
5. The student should clearly understand the concept of naive consciousness and the ethical issues that come with helping a person find a new level of awareness.

Part IV. Integrating Foundational and Historical Treatments with the Client.

Each of these questions refer to commonly used techniques and strategies referred to in some depth in the chapter. With each of the responses some attention must be paid to gender issues and cultural issues. At the beginning of each chapter, these issues are summarized.

1. Decisional counseling techniques include the five stage interview, the balance sheet, and Hansen's ILP.

2. Trauma issues of treatment are referred to in Chapters 7 and 8 (psychodynamic) and in 10 (cognitive-Beck). The student should indicate some awareness of the delicacy of these issues and the importance of working with the client in a solid relationship. Ethical practice and awareness of one's limitations are essential here.

3. Jill could be borderline or histrionic in terms of personality style, more likely borderline. The model on pages 189ff can be employed here. The personality disorder/style chart provides a summary of the type of responses you might expect here.

4. The Rogerian question requires a good deal of creativity on the part of the student. I'd especially look for an intelligent response and expect to learn something from the students here. Most important to me is the ability to help the student see "self-in-relation" and the focus of the person-centered interview should not just be on the person, but also on the manfriend, gender issues, multicultural dimensions, and family context.

5. The five-stage assertiveness training model from Chapter 9 could employed here. Watch especially that the students recall multicultural issues.

6. The densensitization hierarchy is presented in Chapter 9.

7. The stress management concepts are presented in Chapter 9, but should be supplemented by ideas from cognitive dimensions of Chapter 10.

8. The RET self-help form or some type of ABCDEF analysis is most appropriate here, the automatic thoughts of Beck, and the concrete reality dimension of Glasser. Anyone of the three would be appropriate. Additional credit for other dimensions of the models presented. Lazarus may be useful.

9. Dealing with loss and questioning a decision after the fact are central to this issue. The way we think about events at this point becomes as important, or more important, than the event as nothing can be done at this point. The issue here is finding positive meanings and "going on" with life. Look for an understanding of this issue in a gender/multicultural situation and the use of Frankl's philosophy and techniques to facilitate development.

10. Look for understanding of family therapy presented throughout the book. Specially, look for integrating total treatment with the family.

Part V. Network Therapy

Chapter 5 and 6 (MCT) and Chapter 13 (Integration) both outline in some detail specifics of integrated network therapy. DCT's overall frame and Lazarus' BASIC-ID also enrich these ideas.

Look for interventions which involve the individual, the family, the associational groups and neighborhood, and key social services. Also, look for sensorimotor, concrete, formal, and dialectic-systemic interventions (see Chapters 4 and 13).

Final Paper: Transcript Analysis

Interview Typescript Due December 16 (last class) with extension automatic to following Monday morning 9:00 am. Please late transcripts under the door of Allen Ivey's office (462 Hills South). **Please keep a xerox copy of your final paper. Almost every year one paper has been lost "under the door."** If you wish to have your paper returned, please leave a self-addressed stamped envelop with the paper. If you have an on-campus address which uses campus mail, we don't need stamps.

We are asking to audio record an interview of at least 30 minutes in length. We'd like you to transcribe in typescript form at least twenty minutes of the session. Take the most interesting part of the session for you. Transcribe the leads of both you and the volunteer client. If you wish conduct a family or group interview.

Rationale for Assignment: How it May be Helpful to You
Looking at one's own professional style and practice is basic to effective helping. It truly helps to look in detail at what one has done. Many students in this course have used this assignment as a way to present their professional work and include it in applications for work.

Peer review by other professional colleagues is a critical part of professional practice. In the peer review process, we present our work in detail to other professionals. In this assignment, we are asking you to share your paper with a peer from this class or some other helping professional and obtain their feedback on your work as well. Thus, part of your paper is presenting reactions and feedback from a colleague.

The specifics of this assignment are very similar for those who go for the Diplomate examination in Clinical, Counseling, or School Psychology. The Diplomate examination occurs five years after the doctorate is completed and includes a thorough review of the candidates clinical work. An impotant part of the examination is the presentation of a personal transcript of an entire interview with theoretical rationale, transcript analysis, and requires that one be able to criticize one's work.

Outline for Your Paper
Step 1. Planning Plan to conduct an interview with a member of your group, a friend, or an actual client. This interview should last at least 30 minutes (although many prefer a longer time). We at this point are interested in your ability to present an interview and to examine your own behavior and the impact of the interview on the client.

Be sure you have your role-played or volunteer client's permission to record the session. If you are relaxed about taping, your client most likely be comfortable as well. Audiorecord or videorecord the interview. Your client should be free to say at any point that he or she does not want the tape used. Feel free to turn the tape off in the middle. **If you are relaxed about taping, your client most likely be comfortable as well.**

Step 2. Generate a Transcript Develop a twenty-minute (or more) transcript of the session. Place the transcript in a format similar to that described below in Step. 3.3.

Step 3. How to Present the Transcript and your Analysis
Step. 3.1. Begin the presentation to us with a short one page description of the client. **Do not use the client' s name - either leave the name blank or make-up a substitute name.** Indicate on this page that the client gave permission for you to use the material. Please indicate the client's culture and/or primary ethnic background. Do not forget that a European-American background is a culture just as is African-American, etc. Also, recall that gender is a co-culture. (Other co-cultures include age, affectional orientation, religion, area of the country, physical ability, etc.) Please recall that cultural interaction is occuring throughout the interview even if you and your client exist in the same set of co-cultures.

Step 3.2. If you start in the middle of the session, tell us briefly what happened before you actually show us the transcript.

Step 3.3. Present the transcript as follows. Just classify the helpers leads (i.e. you). If you use a skill we haven't covered, do your best to classify it nonetheless. **Note that focus of your lead and confrontation are now added to the classification system. Both skills always appear within the framework of other skills. Also add developmental level classification for both client and counselor.**

9. Al: Before we begin, I'd like to ask if I can tape-record this session. do you mind?
(Closed question, focus on topic, concrete)

Comment: It is very important to make sure clients give you permission to use their words.

10. Jane, Not, that's Ok with me. (concrete)

11. Al: Could you tell me what you'd like to talk about today?
(Open question, focus on client) This is one of those few questions which really doesn't have a specific cognitive-developmental level—it is designed to be open.)

12. Jane: Well, I guess there's lots of thing. I went through a difficult divorce and it was hard on the kids and myuself and we've pulled ourselves together. The kids are doing better in school and

I'm doing better. I've . . . ah . . . got a new friend. (breaks eye contact) But you know, I've been teaching for 13 years and really feel kind of bored with it. It's the same thing over every day --- parts are OK, but I'm bored with it. (formal, dialectic systemic)

13. Al: You say your *bored* with it? (Encourage, focus on client) Formal because you can't see hear.feel, or touch a "bored." Concrete would be "new friend," "13 years" specific concrete things.

(Comment: I noted the eye contact break when Jane talked about her new friend - I thought it might be important, but I decided to wait for awhile before talking about that issue. Also, the last thing a client says in a long string at the beginning of a session is often important to them, thus I focused on that feeling of boredom as I started.)

Note in the above that you are asked to: 1) provide typescript of client and counselor statements, 2) classify your interviewing leads using the microskill framework including focus and confrontation, 3) define cognitive level of both client and counselor statements and 4) make comments about the client and yourself as you go along. Include non-verbal observations. You don't have to comment on each lead, but show that you can look at your work and the interview and make some sort of evaluation and commentary on what you are doing.

Step. 3.4 Identify the specific stages of the interview as you move through them. Note that you may not always follow the order sequentially: indicate clearly that you have returned to Stage 2 from Stage 4 if that occurs. Please try to include some effort at generalization and take-home from this session.

Step. 3.5. At the conclusion of the transcript, provide a brief summary of what happened later in the interview if you don't continue to the end.

The following steps emphasize analysis of your work.

Step. 4.0 **Skill Count..**Provide a skill count for each stage and comment briefly on your use of skills. We anticipate that this time you will be using some influencing skills, but that isn't necessary.

Step 4.1.**Follow-up** Follow-up your interview a week later with a call to your client to find out whether the generalization stage was effective. Did your client do anything differently because of your work together? You may *also* want to ask your client immediately after the session for feedback.

Step. 4.2 **Cultural issues.** Culture exists in each session, even when you share similar co-cultures. European-American U.S. middle-class operates on certain assumptions just as Puerto Rican middle-class operates on certain assumptions. How were culture or co-cultures manifested in the interview? How did the gender of the client relate to the issue? If you wish to consider other co-culture issues, that would be welcomed.

Step 4.3 **What theory of interviewing are you operating under?** You as a helper area already operating on some theory of how people are and what is effective in the interview. Give some attention to your own construction of the helping process and your own rationale as to what you think you would like to see happening in the interview.

Also, as part of this discussion, consider how the client's family of origin might have affected the interview. Keep in mind that the simple question which involves a dual focus *What happens for you when you focus on your family?* This helps the client see her or himself from a family perspective as well.

Step 4.4 **What are your strengths? What did you do right? How can you build on them? In what areas would you seek further development?** In our experience, many students spend all their time criticizing themselves. Pay some attention to what you are doing right! It is on your strengths that you will ultimately become an effective counselor or therapist.

Step 5.0 **Long-term treatment plan.** Assume you are seeing this client in long-term treatment, generate a one or two page treatment plan. Our belief, by the way, is that such treatment plans need to be generated in consultation with the client. Such treatment plans form a contract for your future work together and may be modified jointly with the client periodically. We like to think of the client as "co-investigator" with us in the tradition of feminist therapy and MCT.

Step 6.0 **Peer evaluation.** Ask a peer from the class or an external professional to read your paper and write a commentary in the margins and/or at the end. Recall that we learn most as we share who and what we are with others.

Step 7.0 **Do your want your transcript returned with comments?** If so, please enclosed a self-addressed stamped envelop with correct postage. We will return transcripts by mail to ensure security and privacy.